The Circle

Poetry of Diaspora in Silicon Valley

Jyoti Bachani, Editor

The Circle

Poetry of Diaspora
in Silicon Valley
Volume 3

Disclaimer: This anthology is a compilation of poetry and artwork of diverse individuals. This book does not intend to disrespect any community, caste, religion, creed, nationality, or gender. Copyrights of each contributor's artwork, written words, and poetry remains perpetually with individual contributors while the book as a whole remains copyrighted by the press of which no part, other than attributed excerpts in book reviews, may be used or copied without explicit written permission.

Copyright © 2023 All Rights Reserved
First Edition, First Printing — December 2023
Library of Congress Control Number: 2023948318
ISBN 978-1-953136-63-3   Paperback
ISBN 978-1-953136-69-5   Hardback

Jyoti Bachani, **Editor**
Cover Artwork by Moitreyee Chowdhury
Cover Design by **Pierian Springs Press**
Title Page *Bauhaus Dessau* **Alfarn** by Céline Hurka,
Elia Preuss, Flavia Zimbardi,
Hidetaka Yamasaki, and Luca Pellegrini.
Body text set in URW **Baskerville**
Misc. in **Jenson** by Robert Slimbach & **Sabon** by Jan Tschichold.
Flourishes, Emigre Foundry **Dalliance**, Frank Heine
Adobe Devanagari, Fiona Ross, Robert Slimbach, Tim Holloway
Typefaces licensed Adobe Inc, Linotype Inc, URW GmbH

PSPress.Pub
Pierian Springs Press, Inc
30 N Gould St, Ste 30
Sheridan, Wyoming 82801

Foreword

On the afternoon of the 4th of December in 2016, a few friends from **South Bay Improv** group met in my living room for the soft launch of our friend Lara Lenta aka Madhura Bhakti's poetry book THE SEARCH FOR GOD WITHIN. Most of them were coming to my home for the first time, and to make it easier for them to find my place, Lara Lenta made up a paper sign "Poetry" and pinned it to the tree at my doorstep. That journey, of supporting poets and poetry lovers, has led to this third anthology of poems, among many other delightful poetry adventures. Many poetry lovers are now treated as old friends, some of whom have declared me the founder of **'the Poetry of Diaspora in Silicon Valley"** group that, IMO, is a poetry incubator.

During the Covid pandemic, our monthly meetings went online and became weekly. After spending two to five hours every Saturday night getting high on poems, for fifty two weeks, I decided to create the first anthology, **A MEMORY BOOK OF POETRY OF DIASPORA IN SILICON VALLEY**. I needed a tangible reminder I could hold to make it all 'real.' When the weekly readings lasted another year, the second anthology called STARRY NIGHTS was created in partnership with Pragalbha Doshi, for editing, and Kurt Lovelace, for producing a professionally printed book through **Pierian Springs Press**. Moitreyee Chowdhary provided the cover art for both of those books and volunteered with a "I have to do the cover for this one too!" when we started work on this in September 2023. Kurt Lovelace gave the book its title, THE CIRCLE. I agreed immediately, since we call our meetings **The Poetry Circle,** as my hosting is inspired by my experiences in the Awakin Circles of ServiceSpace.

These anthologies are as much for ourselves as for the unknown reader who might discover a poem that makes their day. Each anthology has poems in multiple languages, some with translations. Each poet contributes what is heartfelt. We leave the door open for everyone, although what we do is not for everyone. We enable and support those who are at ease with their own unique creative voice, and get joy from connecting with others, to co-create in an atmosphere of trust and regard for generous differences. The poems are not screened to fit a theme. The reader is offered a series of poetic adventures, be it delightful, confusing, or not-knowing, and all the rasas that make life worth living.

In a circle, there is no beginning and no end, just a continuous connection. An example illustrates this. Many moons ago, India based poet Anil Karmele, had found me on Meta, where I often translate some contemporary Hindi poetry. Anil sent me some of his poems to translate. Many of Anil's poems are untranslatable. Yet, the few I do translate allows me amongst poets in this anthology, and to bring Anil's Hindi poems to new readers. I am a poetry lover, a poetry translator, a poetry enabler, and a bridge builder using words. Hosting poetry circles and creating these anthologies is my small way to create my world—as I want it to be—a collaborative, productive, poetic and satisfying one.

For the sake of our poets, I wish to record some of the many ripples beyond the circle. In 2020, **India Currents** editor, Shrishti Prabha, invited me to be the poetry editor for this arts and culture magazine that I have admired since the late 1980s. With a monthly column in the magazine, I enabled many of our poets to write their first articles about their love for poems. As they grew in their creative confidence, I also found public forums for us to read poems in the community. For three years now, we have read at the annual **Cupertino Diwali mela**. This year we read at the **Cupertino Poet Laureate** and **Belmont Poet Laureate** events, at the **San Jose Arts Festival**, and the **Mosaic America Festival**. We have also co-created our own online programs, available on YouTube: in 2021, *Irshaad*, led by Sundeep Kohli and family, in 2022, *Mukkarar*, co-created by Praghalbha Doshi with tech support from Prima Virani, with help from Sundeep and me, in 2023, *Navarasa*, sponsored by **India Currents Foundation**. Thanks to Kurt Lovelace, our meticulous publisher, STARRY NIGHTS earned the number one rank on the Amazon best-seller list for the specific category of *South Asian poetry*. Another of our poets, Farooq, was published (in my English translation of the original poem Azaadi) in an anthology WELL EARNED, by **Hawakal Publishers**, to mark the 75th anniversary of Indian independence.

Our traditions of a summer picnic in my garden, the festive potluck after the performance at the Diwali mela, and several invitations from community spaces are now a normal part of our calendars. At our last

Mehfil, our regulars were joined by the former poet laureate of San Mateo county, Lisa Rosenberg, the current poet laureate of Santa Clara county, Tshaka Campbell, along with some first time poetry lovers. Our mehfil favors a vibrant and ongoing conversation in verse with all the warmth of authentic self-expression, over the performative aspects of reading poems out loud. I fancy that we are reclaiming the ancient oral traditions of humans listening to each other patiently, even as we inhabit the digital multimedia world of Silicon Valley.

May you, dear reader, find a taste of delight from this labor of love. My personal tastes favor the discovery of ancient Sanskrit stories that Navneet Gallagali translates, the complex layers of visual imagery in Jai Polepalli's verses, the pure meditation on words from Gerardo Flores, the global expression of Vishal Vatnani, and teasers in languages foreign to me. But as an editor, I do not impose my tastes. The poems are not screened to fit a theme. The reader is offered a series of poetic adventures, be it delightful, confusing, or not-knowing, and all the rasas that make life worth living. The views expressed are owned by the individual poets. I trust that our poets do not intend to harm or offend anyone. We make time for poems while committed to full time occupations, as scientists, professors, doctors, therapists, yoga teachers, etc and juggling roles as mothers, fathers, husbands, wives, sons, daughters, lovers, seekers, friends, etc. This poetry circle makes my world meaningful and fulfilling. May it spread some goodwill to connect and inspire others on their own creative journeys.

Thanks to each of the contributors and to our **Pierian Springs Press** ambassador, Kurt Lovelace, for all the labor of love. Any errors and omissions will be corrected in the next iteration, if you bring them to our attention, and we trust you will be kind and forgiving towards them.

Jyoti Bachani
California, November 2023.

Contents

Salma Arastu

    Ocean of Humanity..3

    Light Upon Light..4

    Bounties from the Bay...5

    Before I see you!..6

    I Am Missing You Today...7

    O Tree..8

    Interconnected Life...9

Jyoti Bachani translates Anil Karmele

    अनुवाद..13

    तुम्हारा मौन..14

    रोना..15

    तकिया..16

    थकान...17

    पीड़ा...18

    नमक..19

    इंतज़ार..20

    बाकी...21

    तुम्हारी अनुपस्थिति..22

    चाह..23

    तुम्हारा साथ...24

    दुःख..26

    हमेशा बाकी...27

    रिक्त..28

Moitreyee Chowdhury
    We? 33
    In the Museum 34

Shruti Dixit
    On Anxiety/Faith 37
    All in a Moment at Sunol 38
    On Needing Validation 39
    Saturday mornings 40
    Guest 42

Pragalbha Doshi
    There is a Difference 45
    Life Pulse 46
    When Peace Eludes 47
    What Do I Really Want? 48
    Trust & Surrender 50

Gerardo Flores
    To Onitsura's Nightingale 53

Navaneet Gallagalli
    The Good and the Bad 57
    Oppenheimer Quotes the Bhagavad Gita ... 58
    Srngara Shatakam 59
    Vairagya Shatakam 60
    Sometimes little is plenty 61
    The birth of poetry, Valmiki 62

Reena Kapoor
    The Smuggler 67
    Liminal Suspension 70
    Locked Out… Or In 73
    Money Grows on Trees 75
    In My Kitchen at Midnight… 77

Sundeep Kohli
    ज़मीं अपनी है 81
    दुआ 82
    ग़ज़ल 83

Faezeh Koohestani
    Surrender 87
    Choice 88
    Grateful 89

Vaishali Kulkarni
    झिंग (Marathi) 93
    नशा (Hindi Translation) 94
    ऋतुचक्र (Marathi) 95
    ऋतुचक्र (Hindi Translation) 97
    निवडुंग (Marathi) 100
    कवी आणि कविता (Marathi) 99
    गुलमोहर (Marathi) 102

Lalit Kumar

    Coming Back to Big Sur 107
    A Santa Barbara Sunset 108
    Joshua Tree of Mojave 109

Kurt Lovelace

    お行儀 | Etiquette 113
    Arbol | Tree 114
    İstanbul'da Yön Bulmaya Çalışmak 115
    Fabulae | Fable 116
    Au Cas où vous Obtiendriez cette Note à Temps 117

Elham Malik

    The Nāsadīya Sūkta (Sanskrit) 121
    The Nāsadīya Sūkta (English) 122
    Poem Inspired by The Nāsadīya Sūkta 124
    Born of The Eternal Fire of Consciousness 126
    Bards of Divine Wisdom 128

Prerona Mukherjee

    Thanatophobia 133
    Immigrants Lament 135
    Dreams 137
    The Eucalyptus Tree 138
    In the moment 139

Jai Polepalli

    अपोह 143
    जूतों का शबिस्तां 144
    अफ़सुर्दा 145

Vidur Sahdev

- The Sea 149
- The Road Ahead 151
- The Flower 156
- Honey 158
- My Honey Bee 160
- The Last Poem 162

Asif Shahid

- One 167
- Two 168
- Three 169
- Four 170
- Five 171
- Six 172
- Seven 173

Topaz

- Grace 177
- Phantom Prophet 178
- Leaves Rustle, Heavy is the Root of Light 179
- The Power of Monks 180

Vishal Vatnani

- Something about the evening 185
- Beautiful faces 186

The Circle

Poetry of Diaspora in Silicon Valley

Salma Arastu

As an internationally exhibited woman artist, she brings a unique global perspective, having been born into the Sindhi and Hindu traditions in Rajasthan, India, and later embracing Islam and moving to the United States in 1986. As a woman, artist, and mother, she works to create harmony by expressing the universality of humanity through paintings, sculpture, calligraphy, and poetry. Her works are greatly influenced by her studies and experiences in different cultures around the world. After graduating in Fine Arts from **Maharaja Sayajirao University** in Baroda, India, she lived and worked in Iran and Kuwait, where she was exposed to a wealth of Islamic arts and Arabic calligraphy. Calligraphy, miniatures, and the folk art of Islam and the Hindu tradition continue to influence her work today.

As a visual artist, she has exhibited her work in over forty-five solo shows nationally and internationally, and won several prestigious awards including the **East Bay Community's Fund for Artists** in 2012 and 2014 and 2020. The City of Berkeley's **Individual Artist Grant Award** in 2014, 2015, and 2016. She has public art pieces on display in Bethlehem, Pennsylvania and San Diego, California. As an author, she has written and published five books of poetry. Her most recent work, on ecological consciousness from Quranic verses, is *OUR EARTH: EMBRACING ALL COMMUNITIES*.

Ocean of Humanity

Do not lose faith in humanity!
It is a vast, limitless, spread-out ocean
It does not get dirty with a few drops of dirt at one end
Or at the other end,
Look at the sparkling waves gushing forward to cover it!
No evil human powers can destroy its beauty
They only cry for our attention
And invite us to advance with force and dignity
Do not shake with fear at a mere bomb blast
Or several gun shots
Rise with determination like these waves
Do not stop, as these are only warnings sent in lots
Move with intention to clean and heal
The naked wounds of humanity
Do not blame the ignorant ones
They are part of this humanity
To test our empathy
Live with patience and power to heal
Within you,
Humanity is an ocean, life-giving and eternal
Can a few drops of evil destroy this glorious unity?

Light Upon Light

When the veil of darkness disappears from your heart
You can visualize within,
A shimmering light!
With the glow of that light
You are able to help your friend, your neighbor.
Remove the dark veil of ignorance and fear.
From their hearts and minds
And as they turn towards their friend.
Igniting their pilot of light
My friend that is light upon light!

Bounties from the Bay

I receive every day
And I fill my pockets,
Collect them with both my hands
Open my heart, mind, and soul
To receive this abundance!
As new hope rises on the sky
Peace and joy start pouring from the dawn
Love and solace
New energy enveloping me from rushing waves
New song emerging from the chirping birds
Inspiration to remain grounded and firm
From the still rocks and trees
Incentive to keep moving as I
Walk with the soft breeze
I return with more than I can hold
It spills on my entire day!

Before I see you!

As I am arriving closer to the end of my life
The point where I do not know what is beyond
I want to stop and fulfill my promises
To heal each soul with my love,
Removing the differences among humanity,
To save Mother Earth and her dignity,
Nurture each plant and creature
With care and sympathy,
Let me take my pen and brush
And bring forth my voice with force
That tears the layers of ignorance
Holding each one in my embrace…
Oh, my Lord!
Help me fulfill my covenant with you.
Before I face you!

I Am Missing You Today

Ama, you taught us from
Vedas and Guru Granth Sahib
Quoting verses of unity and brotherhood
We were told God is surrounding us so
Never do wrong to others
I heard stories of the partition when.
You came holding your children with Baba,
From Pakistan to India as refugees
But you never complained!
And became the sole strength for our family.
Baba left us too early,
But I grew up in your arms,
You poured your spirituality into me.
Ama, I am torn today!
As I hear the stories of racism and enmity increasing
Killing and looking down upon other souls
Dominant races denying all truths,
Narrowing down the vision of a vast Universe
You showed me India as the land of Rishi Muni
Pious Ganges and Yamuna's shores
Himalaya's height to aim,
And depths of Indian Ocean to own,
Broadened vision and accepting all,
Hindus, Muslims, Christians, rich or small
Love for God and love for all
Ama I am missing you today…

O Tree

When I saw you in that fiery orange light
You appeared as black burnt wood
Wildfires are burning your sisters
Were you mourning?
Sun is behind the layer of orange
Smoke has filled the air
I want to save you
Preserve you
Sing with you
Recreate you in my art
My memory is etched
In solidarity with your family
I will grieve with you
And grow more trees…

Interconnected Life

We are all connected together
With single thread of ecology
It is the wisdom of the Ancients
And it was ordained by Universe
We must surrender and sacrifice
To help sustain all
When this connection is unbalanced and
We pull ourselves out from one end
We create entanglement and chaos
It is our destiny…
From the deep earth emerges
Mycelia a life-giving network
White, invisible, and fragile
It spreads,
Rises to the roots of the trees
Growing forests and plants that sustain
All animals and all human life
On this earth and binds us all

Jyoti Bachani

Dr. Jyoti Bachani is a poetry lover who has translated over 120 Hindi poems to English, edited two poetry anthologies, and a special poetry issue of *Journal of Organizational Aesthetics*. She has read at the **Cupertino Poet Laureate** events, the San Francisco *Lit Quake*, *London Poet's Church*, the San Jose Art and **Mosaic America** festivals, and half a dozen annual **Academy of Management** conferences in the US and India.

From 2020-2022, she curated a poetry column for *India Currents*, a Silicon Valley based arts and culture magazine, and also wrote numerous articles about poetry as it relates to current events. She is the founder of **Poetry of Diaspora in Silicon Valley**, a poetry incubator, and hosts regular poetry circles in her home and community, to spread the love of poetry. Her day job is as a full professor at **Saint Mary's College** of California, where she professes how to use the arts to humanize organizations. She enjoyed being a **Fulbright Senior Research Scholar**, a decade ago.

Brief Bio of
Anil Karmele
(for the following translations of the **Hindi** poems)

अनिल करमेले जन्म: 2 मार्च, 1965 छिंदवाड़ा (मध्य प्रदेश) शिक्षा: वाणिज्य एवं हिन्दी साहित्य में स्नातकोत्तर संप्रति: सीएजी के अंतर्गत भोपाल कार्यालय में वरिष्ठ लेखापरीक्षा अधिकारी प्रकाशन: सभी महत्वपूर्ण पत्र-पत्रिकाओं-पहल, हंस, ज्ञानोदय, वागर्थ, वसुधा, नयापथ, कथादेश, आजकल, परिकथा, पाखी, समकालीन भारतीय साहित्य, इंद्रप्रस्थ भारती, साक्षात्कार, आजकल, जनसत्ता, शुक्रवार, पब्लिक एजेंडा, आउटलुक, दैनिक हिन्दुस्तान, नई दुनिया, लोकमत समाचार, दैनिक भास्कर आदि में बहुतेरी कविताएँ, सौ से अधिक लेख एवं कुछ समीक्षाएँ प्रकाशित. कविताओं के भारतीय भाषाओं और अंग्रेज़ी में अनुवाद प्रकाशित। कृतियाँ: "ईश्वर के नाम पर" तथा "बाकी बचे कुछ लोग" कविता संग्रह प्रकाशित। चयनित कविताओं का संग्रह शीघ्र प्रकाश्य। पुरस्कार: कविता संग्रह "ईश्वर के नाम पर" के लिए मध्यप्रदेश साहित्य अकादेमी का "दुष्यंत कुमार" पुरस्कार। विशेष: प्रगतिशील लेखक संघ से संबद्ध. संपर्क: 58, हनुमान नगर, जाट खेड़ी, होशंगाबाद रोड, भोपाल–462026 (मध्य प्रदेश) मोबाइल: +91 (0) 83191-13646 ईमेल: anilkarmele@gmail.com

अनुवाद

मेरी भाषा के तमाम शब्द
तुम्हारे मौन के अनुवाद में
असमर्थ हो जाते हैं...[1]

All the Words of My Language

All the words of my language
Translated into your silence
Become incapable[2]

---

[1] Poem by Anil Karmele
[2] Translation by Jyoti Bachani

तुम्हारा मौन

तुम्हारे मौन में भी कई शब्द
खरगोश की तरह दौड़ते रहते हैं
और मैं उन्हें तुम्हारी
मुस्कान की दूब में खोजता रहता हूँ।[3]

Your Silence

Your silence contains many words
Racing around like rabbits
And I search for them in
The wilderness of your smile.[4]

---

[3] Poem by Anil Karmele
[4] Translation by Jyoti Bachani

रोना

पिता ने कहा
रोते नहीं हैं
रोने से नाराज़ हो जाते हैं पुरखे

माँ ने कहा
मन भर के रो लेना
रोने से सारे दुःख झर जाते हैं

मैं माँ के गले लग कर
फूट फूट कर रोया

हँसता रहा पिता के सामने
वे हँसने को ही समझते रहे मेरा रोना।[5]

To Cry

Father said
Crying is not okay
Crying annoys the ancestors

Mother said
Cry your heart out
Crying relieves the pain

I hugged my mother
And cried unrestrained

I laughed in front of my father
Who understood my laugh as my cry.[6]

---

[5] **Poem by Anil Karmele**
[6] **Translation by Jyoti Bachani**

तकिया

मेरी थकान उतारता
यह जो तकिया है नमी से भरा हुआ
इस पर आँसुओं के निशान हैं
धँसी हैं इसमें टूटे स्वप्नों की किरचें

इसमें से रह रह कर
पिछली रातों की सिसकियाँ सुनाई देती हैं।[7]

Pillow

Relief from fatigue
Offered by this pillow, moist
Stained with tears
Stuffed with rays of broken dreams

From it, the occasional sound of
Prior nights' sobbing can still be heard.[8]

---

[7] **Poem by Anil Karmele**
[8] **Translation by Jyoti Bachani**

थकान

हमारे साथ उन यात्राओं की थकान भी होती है
जो हमने कभी नहीं की
बस, जिनके बारे में सोचते रहे।[9]

Fatigue

With us is fatigue of the journeys
That we have not been on
Just, considered often.[10]

---

[9] **Poem by Anil Karmele**
[10] **Translation by Jyoti Bachani**

पीड़ा

जीवन मे अचानक उपस्थित पीड़ाएँ
कितने चेहरों से मेकअप हटाती हैं

तमाम सुख देने वाली आवाज़ें
तसल्ली और हौसले की हथेलियाँ
और आँखों में रोज़ चमकने वाले तारे
अचानक अनुपस्थित हो जाते हैं।[11]

The Pain

In life, the sudden emergence of pain
Erases the makeup off many faces

The voices that give joy
The hands that support to give courage
The eyes that twinkled everyday
Suddenly disappear![12]

---
[11] Poem by Anil Karmele
[12] Translation by Jyoti Bachani

नमक

खुशी कभी अकेली नहीं आती
उसमें एक दुःख भी शामिल रहता है
नमक की तरह.[13]

Salt

Joy never comes alone
It contains a sorrow within
Like salt.[14]

---

[13] Poem by Anil Karmele
[14] Translation by Jyoti Bachani

इंतज़ार

तुम्हारा गहरा इंतज़ार
धीरे-धीरे ऊब
और फिर उदासी में बदल जाता है

एक सीमा के बाद वह
मिलने से ज़्यादा
न मिलने में ख़ुशी देता है।[15]

Yearning

The deep waiting for you
Gradually turns to boredom
And then transforms into sadness

Beyond a limit
More than meeting
Not meeting yields it joy.[16]

---

[15] Poem by Anil Karmele
[16] Translation by Jyoti Bachani

बाकी

जीवन के सारे लोभ और सारी इच्छाएँ
अनचाही शत्रुताएँ और चाही गई पीड़ाएँ
मेरा क्रोध आँसू और मेरे मन की घृणा
मेरी इस देह के साथ
मिट्टी में मिल जाएंगे
बचे रहेंगे बस प्रेम में उच्चरित शब्द

अगले वसंत इसी मिट्टी में
कई रंगों के फूल खिलेंगे।[17]

Remains

All of life's desires and wishes
Not-chosen enmity and chosen sufferings
My angry tears and my heart's disgust
With this body of mine
Will turn to earth's dust

Only the words said with love will remain

Next spring from this earth
Will bloom flowers of many colors[18]

---

[17] Poem by Anil Karmele
[18] Translation by Jyoti Bachani

तुम्हारी अनुपस्थिति

तुम्हारी अनुपस्थिति भी एक जादू है
कि दीवानावार
हर एक में तुम्हें खोजता हूँ
जैसे हर एक में तुम हो शामिल

मगर तुम्हारी गंध
जैसे चन्द्रमा से झरती चाँदनी
मेरी देह में रक्त के साथ बहती हुई

फिर तमाम रोशनियाँ
तमाम खुशबुएँ दम तोड़तीं हुईं।[19]

Your Absence

Your absence casts a spell
Of madness
I search for you in everyone
As if you are present in everyone

But your scent
Like moonlight flowing from the moon
Flows in my body with my blood

Then, the bright lights
Signal the funerals of many scents.[20]

---

[19] **Poem by Anil Karmele**
[20] **Translation by Jyoti Bachani**

चाह

तुम कहती हो
बहुत हुआ
अगले जनम
मैं गौरैया बनूंगी

सच कहूँ. !
मैं भी तुम्हारे लिए
गुलमोहर बनना चाहता हूँ.[21]

Wish[22]

You say
Enough
Next life
I will be a bird

Truth be told!
I too, for your sake
Wish to be a Gulmohar.[23]

---

[21] Poem by Anil Karmele
[22] Translation by Jyoti Bachani
[23] Gulmohar is a common flowering tree in Northern India, beautiful when in bloom.

तुम्हारा साथ

चमकते सूरज
घूमती पृथ्वी
बहती नदी
हवा, अग्नि, आकाश से ज़्यादा
ज़रूरी है तुम्हारा साथ

यह दुनिया वहीं सबसे सुन्दर
जहाँ मिल जाती हैं
हमारी राहें साथ

हमारे प्रेम से बच कर भागते फिरते हैं
इस दुनिया के स्वामी सारे देवता

हमारे प्रेम के बगैर
तीनों लोक और दसों दिशाएँ
अधूरी और बेजान हैं.

इस दुनिया के स्वामी सारे देवता

हमारे प्रेम के बगैर
तीनों लोक और दसों दिशाएँ
अधूरी और बेजान हैं. [24]

---

[24] Poem by Anil Karmele

Your Company

Shining sun
Rotating earth
Flowing river
Wind, Fire, Sky more
Essential than that, is your company

This world is most beautiful
Where our paths
Meet together

Running away from our love are all
Of this world's swamis and godmen

Without our love
The three worlds and ten directions
Are incomplete and lifeless.

The lords of this world, all the Gods

Without our love
The three world and ten directions
Are incomplete and lifeless![25]

---

[25] Translation by Jyoti Bachani

दुःख

कितने दुःख हैं जीवन में
और कितनी कम कविताएँ

कितना गुस्सा है आसपास
और कविता कितनी रूमानी

कितनी बेचैनी है लगातार तुम्हें चबाती हुई
लेकिन कविता में कितनी कम
और कई बार ठीक इसके विपरीत भी.[26]

Sorrow

So many sorrows in this life
And so few poems

So much anger nearby
And poems so tender

So much anxiety chewing you constantly
But so little in poetry
And sometimes the very opposite.[27]

---

[26] Poem by Anil Karmele
[27] Translation by Jyoti Bachani

हमेशा बाकी

तुम्हारे रूप की आभा में
शब्द ठहर नहीं पाते
बहुत कहना चाहता हूँ लेकिन
हर बार कुछ न कुछ छूट जाता है.[28]

Always Remains[29]

In the splendor of your beauty
Words do not wait
I want to say a lot but
Every time something or other remains[30]

---

[28] Poem by Anil Karmele
[29] Translation by Jyoti Bachani
[30] Everytime something or other remains unsaid

रिक्त

हर पूर्णता को
अधूरेपन से गुज़रना होता है
कुछ पूर्णताएँ
अधूरेपन में ही समाप्त हो जाती हैं.[31]

Without

Every completeness
Must pass through incompleteness
Some completions
Culminate at incompleteness.[32]

---

[31] **Poem by Anil Karmele**
[32] **Translation by Jyoti Bachani**

Moitreyee Chowdhury

Moitreyee is a psychotherapist and artist. She is passionate about building a community, that recognizes the beauty of diversity and works towards equity. Moitreyee enjoys meeting friends from across the globe, learning new languages, art, poetry, and wandering amongst tall trees. She seeks to understand the amalgamation of science, literature, arts, nature, and its relationship with the world.

We?

Lost within freeways
Arriving at the gates of land of the free
Welcomed by freeways to everywhere
Home was never found
I saw those living under the freeways
They were like me
Looking for home
Waiting for freeway to take them home
Waiting and making home under the freeway
While we ride over them, looking for our homes
Do they still dream of that home?
Will they ever reach home?
We?

In the Museum

You put my ancestors in a museum
You looted my land,
gathered my ancestor's soul,
you decided to bring them to your other looted land,
my Ganesha,
my Parvati ma,
You put them in a museum.

The lighting is beautiful.
Decorated and well designed.
I bought tickets to see
my Ganesha,
my Parvati ma
living in the museum.

You never took shoes off.
I could not take my shoes off.
My Ganesha,
my Parvati ma,
my ancestors.

Light is beautiful.
I am here with you.
In the museum

Shruti Dixit

Shruti is excited to share her poetry with the world. In writing poetry she experiences magic. For words, lines, whole rhymes flow—not from her but through her. They help her recognize light and she finds herself going back to these poems for herself—in sharing these, she hopes you will find peace and joy—and that they will bring a chuckle. In other life stuff, she's surrounded by an amazing family and the best of friends; and loves nature. This love finds expression as a landscape designer and as a teacher of architectural and landscape design.

On Anxiety/Faith

In many ways on any day,
There are opportunities to create,
A version of ourselves more in faith.
A version of ourselves that is able to surrender
To happenings close by or yonder.
A version of ourselves that is seeking peace
Within and without.
A version that is also able to see—
Peace is very easy,
It just has to be sought out.
Its when you are at your anxious best,
Is it time to go within and reflect.
Its when you are at your anxious best,
Is it time to go within and reflect.
Whether you pray, chant or meditate,
Anxiety arises when there may be lack of faith.
Its at that time we must firm up our resolve
And keep faith in ourselves and the heavens beyond
There's nothing really to be done
Only something to find
Hiding in plain sight
In your heart, is what some call
Jesus and other's Ram—
God's Shining Light

All in a Moment at Sunol

The hills are majestic.
So green, vast and pure.
They beckon everyone to come and explore.
Joining them are eagles roaming the skies.
With their arms out straight and a graceful stance,
They watch over everything and everyone in their mind's eye.
Showing off their gorgeous brown and white,
I look up to see what caught my eye;
Round and round in the sky they fly.
Are they talking, teaching, learning-
Or just in presence and moment dancing the day by?
The half Moon smiles down,
Through cloudless, remarkable sunny skies.
It is embraced below,
By the oak trees and wild grasses that one can see far and wide.
The woodpecker makes it's presence felt.
Along with many other birds whose words and sounds I can't yet tell.
A beautiful breeze grazes against me,
I see flowers and bees and they allow me to just be.
I hear bells and the pitter patter of little dogs' feet.
Trudging along as their owners urge them to keep speed.
Occasionally a hiker walks by,
You can tell by their pace,
If they've just started or are on their way back from these hills close by.
What a treat, what a treasure to be able to Be.
And find peace in a moment in Sunol - it seems to set one free!

On Needing Validation

Why do we sometimes need,
Someone else to tell us,
That we are doing, or have done just fine?
Whether in actions or in body,
We seek validation.
It really is a big weight on the mind.
How then do we lighten this load?
This load which seems to stem,
From a sense of inferiority.
A sense of not being good enough,
Within yourself.
The solution to me, my friends,
Seems to be to tell ourselves,
That our shine and light is the same as that,
Of the universe that we seek to validate us.
There's not much else.
We are okay, we are fine.
In body and in mind.
There is no feat we can't achieve.
Don't take life so seriously.
Let others be,
Let them say.
They will do what they must.
We must only remember…
Validation comes from within.
Not from outside.
Once you validate yourself,
Others will mirror and follow suit.
So do what you must,
Love yourself.
And let go of the need to hear:
Bravo

Saturday mornings

It's a day of repose,
A day of supposed peace.
After the whole week—
A little easy one hopes one can breathe.

There's a notion in the mind,
Of having lots of time.
One sits down with a cup of tea,
And one begins to find,
Numerous pending tasks.

They seem to emerge as moths coming out of the closet,
when the door is opened, and they see the light.

Let the mind list them all out.
Let the tasks all stand in a line and shout.
That limitless perception of time seems to be fading away…
Oh, how will I get everything done?
and there seems to be no easy way.

I sip my tea.
And I smile.
I'm not the one picking.
I'm a leaf.
The wind will blow and who knows where I'll be.

For now, some words seem to flow.
Maybe I'll do yoga. Maybe meditate.
And after that the dishes will find me.
The vegetables might present themselves—
For chopping, stirring, and frying.
The children will wake up—
And their Saturday morning will take over mine.

Whatever you or I do know that we are free.
You may have a list but that's not what you may do or see.
Once in a while, check in with your heart.
Does the hummingbird call or is there a squirrel playing in the leaves that fall?

Oh, Saturday morning—thank you!
You are full of possibilities but right now I'll go back to sipping that tea!

Guest

A guest has come to my home today.
I've laid out some treats,
And I want her to stay.
She obliges in her own unique way.
Sitting and pecking,
gracefully at the seeds on the tray;
Quietly she has her fill.
Looks around, and then trills.
And soon she's on her way.
Leaving behind some seeds on the floor.
And a beaming me.
For in my home office
For a bit here, I had some lovely company.

Pragalbha Doshi

Pragalbha Doshi lives with her family in San Jose, CA, and works as a therapeutic yoga teacher (E-RYT500, yogasaar.com). By bringing alive the nature of existence and the world in relation to life, poetry emerges from her as an expression of awakening and healing. Inspiration and tranquility are two common responses to her writing. She posts regularly on her blog *Infinite Living* at pragalbhadoshi.com. Her poetry appears in various anthologies and Pragalbha co-edited the 2022 anthology STARRY NIGHTS: POETRY OF DIASPORA IN SILICON VALLEY. She also contributes articles to *India Currents* and *American Kahani* magazines.

There is a Difference

There is a difference.
In living to make it look like
To be seen a certain way
To be remembered a certain way
To be talked about a certain way

And

Actually, living the life exactly
As what would be seen and talked about
Only because that is the only way
That is skilled and known to live.
There is a difference.

The difference is
Vexed exhaustion
And
Calm conviction.

The difference is
Unknown inner suffering
And
Chosen wise suffering

The difference is
Mind maddening rush & fall
And
Heart-exalting ebb & flow

Life Pulse

It is a slow-moving subtle force
This one that comes from the source
It is an incessant life pulse
Felt at times as a powerful surge

It permeates through the Being
It cuts through the dense, deeply piercing
It makes all the living very alive
You feel every feeling very live

Itself as so relentless, makes you so too
Joy or pain, no difference in your pursuit
Unimagined moments lead you to a curve
Sometimes hairpin turns that rightly serve

The thrill is not knowing exactly how
A day set out on, as you think now
Would turn out, you just go humbly wow
All miracalised, you simply flow

The awe is in the process of it all
How all of this adventure
Is something really so internal
As you keep finding way through external

When Peace Eludes

When peace eludes
When purpose seems to lose
When perspective is at ruse
When promises don't produce
When possibilities simply refuse

Then give up control
Then give up the crawl up the wall
Then give up the stickiness of it all
Then give up the judgment tall
Then give up the unkindness of it all

When the train is stopped on track
When the brain is blocked on black
When the mind doesn't cut slack
When heart is feeling the break-n-crack

Then the flood of emotions moisten
Then the time is to wait and listen
Then the path as if waiting to glisten
Then the anguish will eventually lessen

When peace eludes
When the turmoil is profuse
When all the trial is in recluse
When the denial is abstruse

Then the calling is from the Being
Then self-compassion is the Seeking
Then the gift is in the simple Breathing
Then love is what helps only from Within
Then more beauty is what breaks Open

What Do I Really Want?

What do I want?
What do I really want?
Everything anyone would ever want
I seem to have it all

Looks like it just fell to my lap
Just I paid with my life for all that
At times allowed my heart to be taken out whole
Be shaped like whatever anyone wanted
Often put back half used and cold

What do I want?
What do I really want?
Everything anyone would ever want
I seem to have it all

Now is the time
To ask for exactly what I would want
Until now I wanted just what everyone would want
Now is the time
To explore exactly what I am here for

My heart feels safe
In the warmth of my ribcage
Embody gratitude for all that I am gifted
Just not willing to stop asking more
Finally, feel worthy to the core

All roles well played
Each and everyone, theirs and mine
To help me realize
It is me and my heart
Forever together in this lifetime

All else just tremendous perfection
Of how we find other in intersection
Keep nurturing our hearts
Knowing deeply "We are One"
Through eternity & this life in all sorts

What do I want?
What do I really want?
Everything anyone would ever want
That is exactly what I want and more

Trust & Surrender

To trust the timing
For the dreams simmering
Just tremendous faith
For what's been intended

No doubt about fruition
Yet no vex or agitation
Just tremendous alignment
For what's to be manifested

A necessary detachment
Before any enactment
What's been asked, like seeds sown
Will be gifted like a reality grown

Surrender to become the fulfilling channel
With such wondrous ease and intensity
What's to be risen through the tenacity
Is the brightest yet humble luminosity

Gerardo Flores

Gerardo Flores is the co-conspirator who gave Jyoti the courage to host regular poetry circles in her home. He dislikes bios and the usual introductions. He loves technology, books, birds, travels, peanut butter, grapes, languages, doodling and poems. He once jumped out of a plane just because he thought he was afraid of doing it. He can sing and dance, and has been known to ask direct questions. His friends consider him the best pal they could ever have. Everyone in our poetry circle loves to hear him read poetry out loud.

To Onitsura's Nightingale

Quiet bird—I asked—what is it like to be filled with song?
And I poured my song into verses until verses bubbled over and ran.
And I poured my verse into the moonlit sky
      until my heart had overflowed.
But, I did not pour my love, and the sleeping bird did not cry.

Sleeping bird—I asked—what is it like to be free in the wind?
And I fell into reveries until I saw everywhere I'd never been.
And I fell into the sunlit sky until I saw everywhere I had.
But, I did not fall in love, and the little bird did not fly.

Little bird—I asked—what's it like to be birdful and green?
And I whistled its song in these stanzas, yet they're only my words,
      not its voice.
And I whittled its wings in a rose branch, yet the grain
      would not yield to my choice.
And I could not carve love into birdfulness, and the quiet bird
      did not reply.

Forget it!   It's just a small, green bird, say I.
And I'll think so 'till it's pointed out that I've just begun to cry.

Navaneet Gallagali

Navaneet is a software engineer in the bay area with a fascination for Sanskrit poetry. As a lamp lights another lamp, joy increases when shared. With this in mind, he makes bite-sized English translations of Sanskrit and Kannada literature with the intention to give connoisseurs an experience of the rasa (essence) in a short span of time. In addition to the print version, you can find his creations on his YouTube channel:

https://www.youtube.com/rasaganga

The Good and the Bad

गुणदोषौ बुधो गृह्णन् इन्दुक्ष्वेडाविवेश्वरः।
शिरसा श्लाघते पूर्वं परं कण्ठे नियच्छति ॥

Just as Shiva shows his moon and keeps the poison suspended in his throat, the wise display and appreciate the good. They don't let the bad affect them but they are not ignorant of it either. They are aware of its existence, but they keep it at a safe distance—just as Shiva keeps the poison suspended in his throat.

Oppenheimer Quotes the Bhagavad Gita

"Now I am become Death, destroyer of worlds"
>*Oppenheimer quotes this line from the Bhagavad Gita."*
>*Verse 32 from Chapter 11.*

कालोऽस्मि लोकक्षयकृत्प्रवृद्धो लोकान्समाहर्तुमिह प्रवृत्तः ।
ऋतेऽपि त्वां न भविष्यन्ति सर्वे येऽवस्थिताः प्रत्यनीकेषु योधाः ॥

I am Time, engaged in the dissolution of worlds—लोकक्षयकृत्प्रवृद्धो
And even without you—ऋतेऽपि त्वां! येऽवस्थिताः योधा
All these warriors you see, सर्वे न भविष्यन्ति—They will cease to exist.
They are all already in the clutches of Time.

Srngara Shatakam[33]

किमिह बहुभिरुक्तैः युक्ति-शून्यैः प्रलापैः
द्वयमिह पुरुषानाम् सर्वदा सेवनीयम् ।
अभिनव-मद-लीला-लालसम् सुन्दरीणाम्
स्तनभर-परिखिन्नम् यौवनम् वा वनम् वा ॥

What is this empty nonsense that passes for life advice?
There are only two things worth doing in life.
The first - Enjoying the exotic, rousing, filled,
aching breasts of beautiful women.
That's one option. If you're not going to do that,
just retire and go live in a forest.

---

[33] In the first millennium, there lived a king named Bhartṛhari. And in the fire of his youth, he wrote a collection of verses called Srngara Shatakam. This is a sample.

Vairagya Shatakam[34]

रम्यं हर्म्यतलं न किं वसतये श्राव्यं न गेयादिकं
किं वा प्राणसमासमागमसुखं नैवाधिकप्रीतये |
किं तूद्भ्रान्तपतङ्गपक्षपवनव्यालोलदीपाङ्कुर-
-च्छायाचञ्चलमाकलय्य सकलं सन्तो वनान्तं गताः ||

Isn't the royal quarter a beautiful abode? Isn't this music distinctly pleasant to the ears? Isn't uniting with my beloved exquisitely satisfying? And yet!—A disoriented moth is drawn to the light of a lamp. The flutter of its wings stirs up a slight wind, from which the flame flickers and its shadow falters. Like the fickle shadow of that flickering flame, all of these pleasures, these sensory indulgences are transient—realizing this, the wise renounce the world and take to the forest.[35]

---

[34] From the verse, it's rather clear to us which one he'd prefer. If we fast-forward a little, the same Bhartrhari, who is now much older, mellowed by age, writes on the same topic in his Vairagya Shatakam.

[35] We notice a vastly different tone in the two verses. It seems Bhartrhari had a change of heart and found his way from sensuality to renunciation.

Sometimes Little is Plenty

उपकर्तुं यथा स्वल्पः समर्थो न तथा महान् ।
प्रायः कूपः तृषां हन्ति सततं न तु वारिधिः ॥

Sometimes something small may be better than something large.
After all, a well may slake one's thirst, though an ocean cannot.

The birth of poetry, Valmiki

The birth of poetry, how did it all start? Sanskrit tradition gives us a story. The sage Valmiki went to the river and he looked around at the nature surrounding him. And just nearby,

तस्याभ्याशे तु मिथुनं चरन्तमनपायिनम् |

He spots a pair of birds making love, completely absorbed in one another. He hears their sweet sounds of pleasure.

As he watches, all of a sudden, a hunter's arrow strikes the male bird and it falls to the ground.

The female bird sees that:

तं शोणितपरीताङ्गं चेष्टमानं महीतले |
भार्या तु निहतं दृष्ट्वा रुराव करुणां गिरम् ||

Seeing the blood-soaked body of her beloved writhing on the ground,
She cries out in a pitiful voice.

The sage witnesses the entire spectacle and is moved with compassion. In that rush of feeling, he spontaneously curses the hunter with what became known as the first verse:

मा निषाद प्रतिष्ठां त्वम् अगमः शाश्वतीः समाः |
यत् क्रौञ्चमिथुनादेकम् अवधीः काममोहितम् ||

May you the hunter never find prosperity,
having killed a bird absorbed in union, separating the pair.

That verse became known as a shloka (a poetic form common in Indian classical poetry), because it came from shoka, which means sorrow in Sanskrit.

शोकः श्लोकत्वमागतः

The shoka was transformed to shloka. Sorrow was transformed; it achieved a metrical form.

Valmiki later goes on to compose the Ramayana, the first epic poem, in that same shloka format. And so began the birth of poetry.

Reena Kapoor

Techie turned writer, Reena Kapoor grew up all over India as an "army brat". That wandering sensibility is reflected in her debut poetry collection ARRIVALS & DEPARTURES: JOURNEYS IN POEMS. Reena's poetry and stories have appeared in *Bluebird Word*, *433 Magazine*, *Literary Yard*, *Discretionary Love*, *Flash Fiction Forum*, *Ariel Chart*, *Tiny Seed*, *Visible*, *India Currents*. Four plays by Reena were produced by *EnActe Arts* in 2021; her latest was selected for *EnActe's* **New Works Festival** stage reading in Sept 2023.

Reena's been a **Citizen Historian** with **The 1947 Partition Archive** collecting oral histories from witnesses of India's Partition since 2011. She graduated with an undergraduate engineering degree from **IIT Delhi** and a Master's from **Northwestern University**. She's worked as a software product professional for 25 years and mentors social enterprises through **Santa Clara University**.

Reena actively blogs at **arrivalsanddepartures.substack.com**. Her photo-art can be found on Instagram at **@1Stardusty**.

The Smuggler

I arrive with so much more than I declare
offering him my meticulous all-caps customs form
keeping tight two suitcases, slapped four times
with labels of the university address underlined
No, I don't have even $1000 in cash
I answer solemnly, then smile, then don't
Where would I even get that?

*

Yessir, only two suitcases to my name
They'll have to suffice to build a whole life
What does he even know of what I left behind?
All he sees is me: riven, anxious, bursting
for the new world where I arrive
with not much to my name, even less to declare
Only two suitcases? He asks again

*

So little to declare in my suitcases with
clothes ironed into self-conscious shields
two pairs of new shoes for places on a paper map
no accounting for the first snow that'll devour them
Will I need to sell the pieces of jewelry my mother
pressed with her tears into my hand?
Tears I won't understand for another few decades

*

Customs guy barks again, *but what else you bringing?*
Any food in there? Suspicion deepens his lines
I assure him there is none. *No, nothing, nothing really*
He slaps my passport back, turns away, lets me pass!
I hesitate to go. So fresh-off-the-plane, I'll come to laugh
Holding dear all tangible goods that cling back to me
No guilt for what I didn't declare, besides my literal baggage

*

I didn't mention the taste on my tongue
which will torture my senses for rebirth
I didn't mention the map of home
imprinted on my skin bursting to build
I didn't mention colors my eyes thirst for
in flowers I've never seen before
I didn't mention that old music that rings
every morning trailing my dreams
I didn't mention the torch I carry
for familiar warmth and touch and love
Sprouting new shoots on my memory tomb
signed with this new world's epitaph
Don't ask an immigrant what she has in her suitcase
She'll surprise you with mounds of denial

*

All that she brings hidden in her are stories of past life threads
And if you did demand it, she couldn't show you anyway
She'd have to tear off her skin, dissect every cell to look
Even then all you'd see is blood and heart and sweat
You still won't locate it, all that resides, persists
Yet everything of the new she will remake in her own way
You'll have to come find her decades later to see…
…what she got away with!

Liminal Suspension

I sigh deeply as I settle to lie suspended in this space.
Embracing found freedom, before the arrival,
and after the departure, I imagine myself lying free and alone in the sky.
Is this happiness or just relief? And a temporary reprieve?
In the sky so high I should be dizzy and deathly blue,
if it were not for this aluminum chamber.
Somewhere over the Pacific racing, flying away
from what feels like a home I used to have to my current "real" home.

*

Some people are afraid of flying, never me.
It does occur to me that this flying metal sac with several
      hundred humans—
fitted in seats and spaces like good little sardines,
who chose to put their faith in one or two fliers of this machine—
could crash and burn, taking us all down in a jumbled mess!
But it has never bothered me; if I had to go this way would not be
      all bad,
I am told I would be unconscious before much of anything struck.
Even "free fall" sounds like it's ...well... freeing!
Plus so many of us together...couldn't be lonely.
I laugh at these wayward thoughts whizzing by! And at the probabilities
of this and the alternatives—what would I do instead? Lead a caravan,
      ride a camel,
or sit demurely on a ship deck for months like they used to?
That latter option sounds like what a writer ought to do!
Oh the letters I would write you—pages and pages from the deck!
      I dream.
Perhaps it's not wise to laugh, no need to tempt fates,
extinguisher voices in my head remind me.

*

Instead, I savor this feeling, this time after the departure
from what used to be a home but now with my lone, aging mother,
I leave behind with worry and fear of counted days and memories.
This time that comes before the arrival to the home I chose, I built.
Neither permanent, nor fixed with loves I chose, but a feeling
called "home"—not the brick and mortar perimeter in my name.
Yet these fifteen odd hours I suspend in this metal balloon untethered,
becomes the most unchained of them all. This collection of cuboids
separated from the outer skies that I watch
      from my window—dark, serene, deceptive.

*

Treasuring this fragile liminal space—tender, temporal, emotional—
      where I rest,
having handed my fate over to the fliers of this bulbous machine.
Lightened in this surrendering of my fate, in how it feels so weightless?
No binding, no questions, no demands, no ambitions, no responsibility
I am forced to just be; succumb without aphoristic vows, as is. Just be,
      just be!
No obligations, no promises, none to be broken, none kept
In my little space where I sleep, eat and watch a screen
      uncluttered, disrobed
from duties, decisions, ambition, demands, bindings of every kind.
Love exacts. Not just fun and games. Love is grief, is pain,
      a hefty price tag.

I'll think about that later, after I land, tomorrow, next time,
    when I'm back...
A suspension, a reminder that this is what it must feel like
    to be unburdened
To give over the reins of your life to another, a kind benefactor
Do we overrate autonomy? I think out loud
The woman in the next seat stares for a moment, until
we both look away confused. Did she agree or was she mocking,
    I wonder?
No. Her expensive, labeled bags tell me she's not wasting time!

*

And I am wondering, wandering again...
Does this thing fly because it's lightened by the decisions
    we finally made?
My brain wags a finger at my obtuse questions...
Bernoulli explained it all—you at least remember that?!
But wait... I wonder if he missed something!
Did he account for us passengers that cut our bindings,
leaving them speedily trailing in the winds?
Is this thing buoyed because we collectively shed our burdens
leaving all that heaviness behind?
For until we land—
And we pick it all up at the baggage claim of burdens.
Sometimes I envy sheep!

Locked Out... Or In

The lock on my mother's home refusing to open.
The key feels wrong, inadequate. Spins, takes a turn, pretending.
The door sturdy, stubborn, steady. Ace mimic of gravity, fate and death.

*

Call the *Dhobi*.[36] He'll unlock it. That steady witness
    in my parents' story.
A search is launched. Dhobi's phone is called. And called. And called.
No one answers. No answers. The *chowkidar*[37] wrings his hands
    at my desperation.

*

He's back from his village…but isn't answering! So unlike him!
Attending to wounds and scars from the village he left behind? I wonder.
Maybe he too needs a day before yielding to this merciless city's
    keys and calls.

*

---

[36] dhobi = washerman; the man who works the family's laundry - wash, fold, iron. No machine except a coal-fired iron is used by him. Shreepal is his name, and he was an integral part of the trusted help at my parents' home, always available in time of need. His kind attentiveness and heart for what's significant will always remain with me.

[37] chowkidar = night watchman or guard at the gate to the apartment complex where my parents once lived.

I know. I've lived up close to that state of suspension
      between two worlds.
Acknowledging his remorse when they'll demand to know where he was,
I leave without entering. Surrendering this last invitation
      to my lost home.

*

I walk out and about and around. My daughter's tears recall her inside.
A perambulation of her home, her abandoned terrace where
      a million flowers unfurled
shamelessly even after she was gone. I'd had THAT goodbye.

*

I close my eyes imagining her inside. Gathering consolation
      photos of the outside.
Locked out in a prison of grief. Locked out from yet another goodbye.
Another key I'll shape from the only substrate I know:
      the memory of love.

*

Days later, I find a bridge among many. Spanning canals of the city.
A single bridge, like the ones I saw in Paris years ago.
Carrying a multitude of locks affixed by lovers.

*

Lovers who threw their keys away!
Claiming their love is all. Locked. Unbroken. For eternity.
I found some answers.

Money Grows on Trees

Young ladies, does money grow on trees?
my father would shake his head to ask.
Rhetorical, as many of the
philosophical questions, he'd
pose to my sister and I.
Usually after we'd presented a
case for a new bauble we must
possess, having depleted our
meager "pocket" money on other
temptations that waylaid our paths.

*

Eager supplicants we'd jump to answer,
for it was, we knew, a jocular exchange.
Such questions meant we were winning.
Sure it does, Papa! Look outside...
At which point he'd peer outside, shaking,
his head, *Ah! I see it now.*
All this banter would pour out from him
as if complaining about our burdens.
Anyone listening would think, what a
penny-pinching father this is!
But they'd have to know us, to know
how far from the truth they'd landed.

*

These were my father's sweet protests
even as he readied to buy the trifles
our insatiable hearts demanded!
Cadbury's Milk Chocolate bars,
Poppins and Chocobars,
Coca-Cola until it was banned there…
Dizzying high heels in our teen years
He'd pay up vigorously rolling his eyes,
How can anyone walk in those?
Or a vinyl record we'd been pining for,
This noise will command the player!
When will I play my ghazals?
he'd lament in mock horror emptying
his wallet to make space for our clamoring.

*

A dream arrived last night in which
I'm smothering his big cheeks
with kisses and he's nodding with
that happy, content warmth I miss.
I woke up smiling in secure captivity
surrounded by a love that lives and
thrives even in these years that come
after his gentle, unassuming passing.
As if he's here, saying, *Give abundantly.*
Little things are big things.

*

The way he lived!

In My Kitchen at Midnight…

In my kitchen at midnight
I coax chickpeas she demands,
the day before she arrives.
I know she likes them sour
and piquant, spicy and rich.
Lining spices, I carry
love, a heavy bottomed pot.

*

I roast *anardana, zeera,*[38]
Tez patta, laung, amchur—young
mangoes once, now powdered dry.
Peel and chop, ready flavors that
blossom over searing flame.
Onions divine tears in
eyes, a worthy camouflage.

*

Multitudes, distractions, calls
but this mastery I can't fail.
No barter, no prestige, no
pay. Still, nothing can subdue
this potent preparation.
I've clasped glories from taller
vantages. None burned so close.

---

[38] anardana, zeera, Tez patta, laung, amchur - Indian spices as in (resp.) dried pomegranate seeds, cumin, bay leaf, clove, dried mango powder.

*

She's in my kitchen. I read
more than hunger. She sees me
ladle caution as I serve,
Why'd you worry for me, Ma?
I laugh, not speak out loud, *You'll
know the day you're disarmed by
a tiny, defenseless one…*

Sundeep Kohli

Sundeep is an engineer by profession and got his Graduate degree in Electrical Engineering from **IISc Bangalore**. He is passionate about Urdu poetry and writes Ghazals and Nazms, on his favorite topics of romance, philosophy, politics and life. His Facebook page is *@shayarsundeep*, where you may read more of his poetry.

He has published poems with **Cupertino Poet Laureates** and with **Poetry of Diaspora in Silicon Valley**. Sundeep is associated with **Kavvya Connection** poetry meet-up and participates in their regular events. He has have also been invited to participate in San Jose poetry circle's **Bauchaar** poetry group, and he has recited his poems in online Mushaira events.

ज़मीं अपनी है

ज़मीन अपनी है अपना आसमान है
फ़क़त इतनी सी अपनी दास्ताँ है

ना जाने कब से चलता आ रहा था
मसलसल वक़्त अपने दरम्यान है

हमारा घर है यह जो जल रहा है
यही धरती हमारी पसबाँ है

कहीं लूटा ना जाए ख़ुद के हाथों
हमारी ज़िंदगी का कारवाँ है

दरख़्तों की कहानी सुन के देखो
दरख़्तों की कहानी बेपनाह है

ज़रूरत की ज़रूरत किस लिए है
तेरे दामन में पूरा गुलिस्ताँ है

तू इस जादू के बंधन से निकल जा
तेरे उड़ने को सारा आसमाँ है

दुआ

सब के अरमान फिर से फूलें फलें
इस दिवाली में दिल का फूल खिले

फिर से मेले हो फिर मसरत हो
तनहा रहने के दिन तो कब के ढले

ना ही शिकवा हो ना गिला कोई
सब को अपनो का प्यार फिर से मिले

शादमानी ही शादमानी हो
प्यार की शम्मा हर नज़र में जले

दिल के सहरा को फ़िर घटा चूमे
तरसी आंखों को कुछ सुकून मिले

ग़ज़ल

मंज़िल से ही मंज़िल का पता पूछ रहा है
इक शख़्स अपने घर का पता पूछ रहा है

गुलदान में डाली से टूटा फूल सजा है
उस गुल से क्यों खिलने की अदा पूछ रहा है

कानों में बहुत दूर तक जो गूंजती रही
ना जाने थी वो किसकी सदा पूछ रहा है

फ़ितरत में पत्थरों की हैं ठोकर की साज़िशें
क्यों इनसे तू ज़ख़्मों की दवा पूछ रहा है

परवाज़ परिंदे को पैदाइश से मिली थी
पर उड़ के अब जाना है कहाँ पूछ रहा है

ख़ुद अपनी रमज़ समझ ना आयी तुझे मगर
क्यों रूठ गया तुझ से ख़ुदा पूछ रहा है

कुछ उस के सवालों की सदाक़त का असर है
ग़ाफ़िल से ख़ुदा उसकी रज़ा पूछ रहा है

Faezeh Koohestani

Fae Koohestani writes in Farsi (Persian) and English. She is a biomedical scientist who spends her time outside of work on reading, painting and writing calligraphy. As a lover of creativity, she enjoys any creative work with words as poems or stories. She sees words like colors as a raw and versatile tool for creatively displaying the experience of being human in the universe. Although she appreciates traditional forms of poetry, she prefers the free style or modern forms of poetry, particularly modern Persian poetry.

Surrender

To receive, form, and nurture;
    only to let go
           into the world of possibilities—
           those with the unfortunate outcomes—
           was how
           she was taught to be a mother.
While wondering if mother birds, kangaroos, and bears
    let go
           into the world of possibilities—*as they come.*

Choice

This is the verge,
> where you place—*with utmost attention*—
> one foot in front of the other.

This is the verge,
> where you place—*with utmost joy*—
> each eon of your awareness
> into the vast realms
>> widely spread on each side of you
>
> inviting you to stray
>> into their bosom.

This is the verge,
> where your aware feet
> dip enough of their toes
> into each realm
>> to keep you submerged
>> into the possibilities of each side,
>>> *and beyond;*
>>
>> where the amalgam of the sides
>> may forever keep you
>>> on the verge.

Grateful

Soft, light, and fresh
    were the tears leaving his eyes
        wondering how they can thank the heart
        who set them on their journey
        beyond his eyes.

Vaishali Kulkarni

Vaishali Kulkarni is a qualified Pharma professional working in medicine and healthcare industry for about 20 years. She is from Maharashtra, India and has immense love for her mother tongue Marathi. Her love towards Marathi gets expressed through her poetry. Though she covers variety of topics in her writing, many of her poems talk about human feelings and relationships and nature. She has created multiple arts of poetry in collaboration with Varsha More under the hash tag *#chitrolivarshalichya* wherein the words by Vaishali and pictures by Varsha complement each other.

झिंग

(Marathi)

मी खेळ मांडला आयुष्या घे पिसून पत्ते नीट आता..
कुठल्या हाती कुठला पत्ता दैवच जाणे डाव आता..

मी पुन्हा एकदा मैदानी बघ हार पचवूनीही शतदा
जर झाले विजयी यावेळी,तर नकोस होऊ शरमिंदा

चल ये असा ये सामोरा ,अन दे नजरेला जरा नजर
चल देते पहिली संधी तुला,तू पहिले आपली चाल कर

मज रडवण्यास नी हरवण्यास तू शर्थ करावी खुशाल रे
मज रोज सकाळी बळ देती ही तुझी आव्हाने मित्रा रे

मज अप्रूप नाही विजयाचे ना अपयश आता छळत मला
बस ठाण मांडूनी लढण्याची ही चढते आहे झिंग मला

नशा

(Hindi Translation)

आ खेले जिंदगी ताष जरा , बांट पत्ते थोडा सोच जरा
किसके हाथ कौन सा पत्ता , कोई न जाने खेल खरा

सौ हार पचाके मैं फिर भी हाजिर हू मैदाने जंग मे
गर हो जाऊ विजयी अब तो ना शर्मिंदा होना मन में

आ सामने तू आ जरा, और मिला नजर से मेरी नजर
चल दिया मौका पेहला तुझे तू पहली अपनी चाल कर

मुझे हराने रुलाने के खातीर तू जोर लगा ले पुरा रे
मुझे रोज सुबह है ऊर्जा देती ये तेरी चुनौती साथी रे

अब विजय मिले या हारू मैं, ना पडता कोई फर्क मुझे
जी जान से डंटके लडनेका चढ जाता है बस नशा मुझे

26 मे 2023

ऋतुचक्र

(Marathi)

ग्रीष्मातल्या झळा त्या
अतिशुष्क दिवस जातो
आकाश जाळ ओकी
अन तप्त देह होतो

ते दान तगमगीचे
पोटातले निखारे
अस्ताचलीही दिनकर
रातीच्या ओंजळी देतो

दिनरात कोरडे ते
माती तहानलेली
आसुसल्या दिठीने
वर्षेस साद घाली

होता कृष्ण कांती
आभाळ दाटलेले
झरती जलधारा
अन तृप्त होई धरणी

प्राशुनी अमृता त्या
मातीस ये सृजनता
गर्भस्थ कोंब फुटतो
पिऊनी जलपान्हा

देऊन दान हिरवे
अवनीस दो भुजानी
वर्षा ऋतुही जातो
घालून शीळ शिशिरा

घेऊन माघ थंडी
अन गार गार वारा
शिशिरातल्या दिनाना
सामावते ती बंडी

ती पानझड ही सारी
गारठून वृक्ष पाही
डोळ्यात ठेवुनिया
मधु स्वप्ने वसंती

येतो वसंत नाचत
बहर बहर रानी
नवपालवी सुखाची
घे लेऊन अवनी

हा खेळ या ऋतूंचा
चाले असाच अविरत
लयबद्ध त्यास ठेका
ठेवी मना जिवंत

ऋतुचक्र
(Hindi Translation)

ग्रीष्म मे चलती ये लुं
दीन जल जाता है यू
आग बरसे आकाश से
तप सी जाती है रुह

ये दान तपिश का व
उदर के अंगारे
अस्ताचल पे सूरज
अवनी का आचल भरे

दीन रात पडे सुखे
प्यासी प्यासी माटी
आस बेहती नजरोसे
बरसात को पुकारे

अंबर भी उमड जाये
हो नभ फिर सावलासा
बरसती जलधाराये
धरती का मन शीतलसा

जल अमृत कर प्राशन
सृजनत्व ओढे ये धरा
गर्भस्थ फले अंकुर
पी कर जलधारा

कर दान भर भर कर
अवनी को ये हरा
वर्षा ऋतू भी चल दिया
शिशिर को कर इशारा

ले कर माघकी ठंडी
और सर्द हवाए कलकल
जाडे के इन दिनो को
समेट लेता है कंबल

वो पतझड भी पुरी
साहे वृक्षकाया ठीठुरती
नयनोंमे संभाले
मधु सपने बसंती

आता बसंत नाचता
बहर बहर हर डाली
नवपल्लवी चूनरिया
अवनीने सरपे ओढली

ये खेल इन ऋतुओंका
अविरतही चला जाता
एक लय जो इनमे है ना
मेरे मन को लुभाता

कवी आणि कविता

(Marathi)

हे कविता बिविता लिहीण अहो
शहाण्यांची कामं नसतात.
यांच्यात पाऊस बोलतो बिलतो
आणि म्हणे तारे हसतात..

थोडा ढील्लाच असतो बहुदा
या कवी लोकांचा आटा
यांना भाकरीत दिसतो चंद्र
आणि डोळ्यांमध्ये लाटा

उगीच त्यांना सारे म्हणतात
बुद्धिवादी न काय काय
हसणाऱ्याला रडवणे हे
शहाणपणाचे झाले काय?

अस काही लिहितात कधी
की काळजात अगदी धस्स होते
कधी कधी उगीचच वाचून
गालावरती लाली येते

अक्कल गहाण असते कवीची
कवितेची मस्ती असते
येतो जो जो संपर्कात त्याची
ब्रह्मानंदी टाळी लागते

शब्दावर जगत असतात नुसते
तहानभूक पण लागू नये?
खर सांगते शहाण्यांनी
कवीच्या नादी लागू नये

29 जून 2022

निवडुंग
(Marathi)

पागोळ्याहून ओघळणारा कुणी थेम्ब तो वर्षेचा
छपरावरुनी मातीमध्ये जन्मच त्याचा निमिषाचा

अन तैसाची थेम्ब दुसरा नक्षले कुणी स्वातीच्या
मेघा मधुनी अलगद पडतो होतो मोती भाग्याचा

कुणी गुलाब फुलतो उद्यानी असतो माळी दीमतीला
फुल फुटतसे खडकामधे काटेरी निवडुंगाला

जरी गोजिरी दोन्ही पुष्पे फुलती काट्या काट्यावर
एक मिरवतो राजा म्हणुनी दुजा सुकतसे खडकावर

एक सारखे नसते कधिही लिहिले सर्वच भाळांवर
वेग वेगळी घेउन नशीबे जीव जन्मती पृथ्विवर

Cactus & Rose buds

Rolling down the roof,
a drop of rain oh so tiny
From the roof into the soil
what a momentary journey

And yet another drop but so lucky
Born in a cloud in nakshatra Swaaty
Oozes down the cloud straignt into a shell
And turns into a precious pretty pearl

Some where a rosebud blooms with a bliss
Sprinkler, manure, gardener all at its service
Same time on a rocky and thorny bed
Cactus gives life to a cute little bud

Shrouded by the thorns though
both of them bloom
While one struts the kinglife
The other dies off gloom

Written with the same ink
is not everyone's fate

गुलमोहर
(Marathi)

रणरणता जरी सूर्य फेकतो उन बापुड्या धरणी वर
वैशाखी ही उन्हात फुलतो मजेत झुलतो गुलमोहर

लालचुटुक भरगोस फुलांचे गुच्छ बाळगत अंगावर
लाल सड्याने पायापाशी गालिचा पसरतो गुलमोहर

नाजूक इवली इवली पाने हिरवी हुळहुळ वाऱ्यावर
मधेच चपट्या लांबट शेंगा कसा फेकतो गुलमोहर

लाल पाकळ्या सर्व तरीही एकच पिवळी जोरावर
असे लाघवी मोहक रुपडे घेउन बहरतो गुलमोहर

कधी खिडकीशी गच्चीवर कधी कधी रस्त्याच्या टोकावर
लाल आपुले बहर घेऊनी मनात फुलतो गुलमोहर

Lalit Kumar

Lalit Kumar lives in San Francisco Bay Area and likes to write both poetry and prose around the themes of adventure and exploration. He currently writes a regular column in *India Currents* magazine sharing his passion for adventure sports. His book **YEARS SPENT: EXPLORING POETRY IN ADVENTURE, LIFE AND LOVE** was among top three **Selects in Poetry** genre featured in *'Indie Spotlight'* by **BookLife** in *Publishers Weekly*, 25th July 2022 edition. His poems have also featured in various anthologies including *Everything Intensely, San Francisco Writers Conference 2022.* Find him on:

Instagram @lalitk06 *or* www.lalitkumaronline.com

His next poetry book is called **YOSEMITE OF MY HEART: POEMS OF ADVENTURES IN CALIFORNIA** due to release in early 2024. These poems are taken from that collection.

Coming Back to Big Sur

A summer dream, to run down
Narrow, winding, coastal Highway 1.
Don't hurry to make love, rather observe
Rising waves carried from ocean deep,
Caress the rugged shore of Big Sur passionately, in rhythmic precision.

Same exact spot where we last made love,
Looking at the tired, roiling sea break upon its thirsty shore.
I tasted your lips within seventeen-mile drive,
I remember the taste of salt and sand,
I remember the humid and craggy Pebble beach.

I reach Bixby Canyon Bridge, the wild beauty,
California Dreaming ringing in my ear
And I think of Kerouac and Miller, loci of inspiration,
And Big Sur crystallizes for me in sharp relief,
Santa Lucia Mountains rise precipitously from the Pacific.

This time I am in no hurry to return home.
I come to see the inlands' redwoods, conifers, sycamores
I watch the mighty condors in the sky, gulls on the boulders
I have come to drink the intoxicating air
Pining for my daydream to manifest in the enchanting Big Sur.

A Santa Barbara Sunset

The sky is awash in golden rays, orange hues
Cast their net wide on the coastal Pacific waters.
The dazzling cliffs on the beach
Take a stance on the breaking waves.
A surfer is quick to paddle out of the rip currents, Campus Point
Comes alive to the gradual, collective beats of its residents.

An evening cruise ship sets its sails in distant water,
      Santa Barbara harbor
Comes home tonight
To its local wines and grand carousals
Swaying palm trees sing of the sea and ancient mariners.
The evening is lit aglow against Santa Ynez Mountain
Sky—mountain and ocean one, giant, tangerine fireball.

Joshua Tree of Mojave

Arid, Mojave desert landscape,
Spartan, feisty under relentless Sun,
Austere rock outcrops, shrubs—
Wildflowers under a clear blue sky
Bloom vividly beneath a thousand stars
Under the cover of cold, dark night.
A solid trunk of a tree, a poetry
Unfurls its branches in a twisted scape,
Gazing straight upon the starry night,
In deep contemplation of its sparse existence.
Eking out a living of its own—
Resilient, the root seeks water through fault-lines of desert
Standing alone in sublime beauty of harsh climes,
Radiates joy to the lone hiker.
In the beauty of a silhouette, it emerges—
The Joshua tree of Mojave.

Kurt Lovelace

An editor, writer, translator, and mathematician, Kurt's work has appeared in **The Lascaux Review**, **North Dakota Quarterly**, **San Antonio Review**, U.K. Lancaster University's **Red Ogre Review**, U.H. Honor College's **Athena** and other journals.

HALFWAY BETWEEN EVERYWHERE is Kurt's most recent collection of poetry, which includes selected translations and essays on poetry. An audiobook is also available. Two new collections, APOPHRADES & INTREPITUDES and DISFIGUREMENTS, are both in progress, and forthcoming.

Of the five pieces included here, **Etiquette, Trying to Navigate in Istanbul**, and **Au Cas où vous Obtiendriez cette Note à Temps** are Kurt's own original compositions, each part of a section entitled **"Polyglot"** in a forthcoming book.

The poem **Árbol** and the prose passage **Fabulae** are Kurt's translations from the original Spanish and Latin texts.

お行儀 | Etiquette

    she lifts up
彼女は箸で寿司を持ち上げる。
       with her chopsticks
           a piece of sushi

    her teeth rip into
彼女の歯は、肉厚のオレンジ色の魚肉を引き裂く。
       thick pulpy orange
          fish flesh

    her fish juice
彼女の魚の汁が私の左目にしみこんで、しみる。
       squirts into
          my left eye, stinging

    the closed slender rose petals
彼女の左手の指は、それぞれ細長いバラの花びらを閉じている。
       of each finger on her left hand
          shields her giggling lips

It is all 全ては very とても Japanese. 日本人です。

Kurt Lovelace

Árbol

Anoche al apagar la luz
se me durmieron las raíces
y se me quedaron los ojos
enredados entre las hojas
hasta que, tarde, con la sombra
se me cayó una rama al sueño
y por el tronco me subió
la fría noche de cristal
como una iguana transparente.

Entonces me quedé dormido.

Cerré los ojos y las hojas.

>   **Pablo Neruda**
>   *(1904-1973)*

Tree

Last night as the last light
left, the roots of me
dozed off but my eyes
strayed, open, tangled in my leaves;
later the shadow of a branch
slipped over my dreams
climbing up onto the trunk
of the cold, pellucid
night, a transparent iguana.

Then sleep came to me.

I closed my lashes and my leaves.

İstanbul'da Yön Bulmaya Çalışmak

Trying to Navigate in Istanbul

    It wasn't the streets that where hard but words
Zor olan sokaklar değildi, kelimelerdi.
seslerin eski çimento parke taşlarında
    ancient cemented cobblestones of voices

    and meanings threaded through carpets faded
ve anlamlar solmuş halıların arasından
heceleri şekillendiren dillerin uzun ayakkabılarından.
    from the long foot-wear of tongues shaping syllables.

    Not knowing which way the wind blows,
Rüzgarın hangi yönden estiği umurunda değil.
Durdu ve bana bakıp şöyle dedi:
    I halt a man, and ask the way to Sultanahmet Square?

Amerikan suratını sikeyim.
    I bowed profusely thanking him.

Fabulae

Cura cum quendam fluvium transiret, vidit cretosum lutum, sustulit cogitabunda et coepit fingere hominem. Dum deliberat secum quidnam fecisset, intervenit Iovis; rogat eum Cura, ut ei daret spiritum, quod facile ab Iove impetravit. Cui cum vellet Cura nomen suum imponere, Iovis prohibuit suumque nomen ei dandum esse dixit. Dum de nomine Cura et Iovis disceptarent, surrexit et Tellus suumque nomen ei imponi debere dicebat, quandoquidem corpus suum praebuisset. Sumpserunt Saturnum iudicem; quibus Saturnus aequus videtur iudicasse: "Tu, Iovis, quoniam spiritum dedisti, animam post mortem accipe; Tellus, quoniam corpus praebuit, corpus recipito. Cura quoniam prima eum finxit, quamdiu vixerit, Cura eum possideat; sed quoniam de nomine eius controversia est, homo vocetur, quoniam ex humo videtur esse factus."

Gaius Iulius Hyginus
(c. 64 BC – AD 17)

Fable

As Care once crossed a certain river, she saw some chalky clay, picked it up, and thoughtfully began to shape it into a figure. As she pondered her work, Jupiter appeared; Care pleaded with him to give it a spirit, and this Jupiter happily bestowed onto it. But when Care wanted her name placed upon it, Jupiter prohibited her, saying that his name must be put on it. As they debated which name it should have, Earth arose and said that it must take Earth's name, since it had provided the body. So, to arbitrate, they invited Saturn to be the judge; whereupon Saturn appears to have judged very equally: "You, Jupiter, since you gave it spirit, you shall receive its sprit upon death; Earth, since you provided its body, you shall receive its body. And as Care first formed it, Care shall posses it all of the days of its life; but as to the controversy over its name, it shall be called Homo, for it is made out of humus *(earth)*."

Au Cas où vous Obtiendriez cette Note à Temps

A l'heure qu'il est, vous avez déjà mangé
la succulente pêche froide
que j'avais rangée au fond du frigo,

dont vous avez probablement pensé
que je gardais
pour mon petit déjeuner.

Pardonnez-moi. Il ne fait aucun doute que votre bouche
l'a trouvé délectable, léchant des lèvres humides
si douces et si

empoisonnées.

In Case You get this Note in Time

By now you've eaten
the cold succulent peach
I'd stashed back of the frig,

of which you probably
thought I was saving
for my breakfast.

Forgive me. No doubt your mouth
found it delectable, licking wet lips
so sweet and so

poisoned.

Elham Malik

Elham Malik is an ardent researcher at the core of her being, a scholar whose passion extends to poetry, hymns, and ghazals. She relishes the art of crafting verses in ways that are not only innovative but also resonantly aesthetic. Her heart finds solace in delving into the boundless universe of poetry, seeking to uncover the enigmatic and unspoken sentiments concealed within the hearts of poems. This self-expression nourishes her soul and harmonizes with her scholarly pursuit in the domain of Organizational Behavior at the illustrious **Indian Institute of Technology**, Banaras Hindu University. Amidst the intellectually and spiritually fecund environs of Varanasi, Elham luxuriates in her exploration of poetic masterpieces in a kaleidoscope of languages, akin to marveling at the vibrant hues of a rainbow.

The Nāsadīya Sūkta
from the **Rigveda** (10:129) (Sanskrit)

नासदासीन्नो सदासीत्तदानीं नासीद्रजो नो व्योमा परो यत् ।
किमावरीवः कुह कस्य शर्मन्नम्भः किमासीद्गहनं गभीरम् ॥ १॥
न मृत्युरासीदमृतं न तर्हि न रात्र्या अह्न आसीत्प्रकेतः ।
आनीदवातं स्वधया तदेकं तस्माद्धान्यन्न परः किञ्चनास ॥ २॥
तम आसीत्तमसा गूळ्हमग्रे प्रकेतं सलिलं सर्वाऽइदम् ।
तुच्छ्येनाभ्वपिहितं यदासीत्तपसस्तन्महिनाजायतैकम् ॥ ३॥
कामस्तदग्रे समवर्तताधि मनसो रेतः प्रथमं यदासीत् ।
सतो बन्धुमसति निरविन्दन्हृदि प्रतीष्या कवयो मनीषा ॥ ४॥
तिरश्चीनो विततो रश्मिरेषामधः स्विदासीदुपरि स्विदासीत् ।
रेतोधा आसन्महिमान आसन्त्स्वधा अवस्तात्प्रयतिः परस्तात् ॥ ५॥
को अद्धा वेद क इह प्र वोचत्कुत आजाता कुत इयं विसृष्टिः ।
अर्वाग्देवा अस्य विसर्जनेनाथा को वेद यत आबभूव ॥ ६॥
इयं विसृष्टिर्यत आबभूव यदि वा दधे यदि वा न ।
यो अस्याध्यक्षः परमे व्योमन्त्सो अङ्ग वेद यदि वा न वेद ॥ ७॥

The Nāsadīya Sūkta
from the **RIGVEDA** (10:129) (Sanskrit)
Translation by **Elham Malik**

Prior to the dawn of creation
Neither was there existence nor the non-existence
Nether was there the element of air nor the ether
Even nothing was beyond the then non-existent air, ether and soil
The only element existent was darkness
The darkness as grave and fathomless as the then non-existent oceans
Then, neither was the existence of death nor the immortality
Then, neither was the existence of mortal humans nor
      the immortal heavenly beings
Then, neither was the existence of day nor the night
The only existent entity then was the 'Perpetual Substance',
      the 'Prakriti'
This perpetual substance has neither any beginning nor the end
In the dawn of the creation there was only the darkness
      shrouded by darkness
The 'Perpetual Substance' was fluid like water that could take
      any form or dimension
Out of the incessant great penance in this 'Perpetual Substance'
      emerged the supreme soul
The supreme soul 'Parmatman' who is the creator of this creation
      'the apparent universe'

The seed of creation was the desire of the 'Parmatman'
This desire paved the way on the wedge that separated
    existence and non-existence
From the seed of the desire of creation emerged the luminous
    streaks of light beams
The light beams as bright as sun beams representing the part
    of supreme energy
These light beams merged with the perpetual substance 'Prakriti'
    to give birth to the creation 'Srishti'
Even the most enlightened of all beings were born after
    and from the creation
Therefore, even the enlightened ones do not know how exactly
    the world was created
Where exactly did all we see, hear, touch, feel, and witness come from?
No existent entity can tell with certainty what existed before
    the dawn of creation.
Nor can they tell accurately what was the reason for the creation
    of everything that exists
What is the source of creation?
Who is the doer of all that happens in this creation?
Who operates this creation?
Who overviews this creation?
Is he the one perceiving all the activities in this creation
    sitting high in the skies above us?
Or maybe even he doesn't know the secret of creation.

A Poem Inspired by The Nāsadīya Sūkta

Before the dawn of creation's light,
No existence, nor the void's endless night,
Neither air nor ethereal heights,
In the realm where nothing met the sight.

A darkness shrouded, deep and wide,
As boundless as oceans, in its stride,
No death, no life, no celestial guide,
No day, no night, the void did bide.

In this eternal, formless sea,
Lay the 'Perpetual Substance,' mystery,
No beginning or end, it's meant to be,
In creation's dawn, it yearned to see.

From this Substance's ceaseless flow,
A supreme soul began to grow,
'Parmatman,' creator, pure and aglow,
Crafted the universe's grand tableau.

Desire's seed, in the cosmic dance,
Spanned the gap between chance and chance,
Light beams radiant, a celestial lance,
Merged with 'Prakriti,' in a sacred trance.

From this union, the universe sprung,
Life and matter, like a song unsung,
Even the enlightened, with wisdom, hung,
Know not how creation's veil was flung.

Whence came all we see and know,
The source from which life's rivers flow,
The puppeteer of this grand show,
In the heavens high or down below?

The secret of creation, none can tell,
In this cosmic drama where we dwell,
A riddle that even the heavens dispel,
The mystic tale no one can unveil.

So, who orchestrates this cosmic flight,
Who oversees the day and night?
Is it a presence distant from our sight,
Or even they may not grasp the light?

In this grand enigma's endless gyre,
The secret of creation remains entire,
A cosmic mystery burning like fire,
In the heart of existence, we inquire.

Born of The Eternal Fire of Consciousness

In the realm where whispers of love do flow,
Yet, on the tumultuous path we often go,
In every corner of the lover's heart, the beloved's name shines,
On pages of life, the flame, the lover, becomes the holy shrine.

Till one's consumed by love's eternal fire,
The divine's true essence, one cannot admire,
For love itself is supreme, a force untamed,
Its repercussions, too, in our souls are deeply framed.

Once love's sweet touch graces the souls,
Unloving becomes a distant, far-off goal,
Neither living nor dying, the lovers exist in grace,
Thriving to fulfill compassion's divine embrace.

The beloved's promises, a cost all lovers choose to bear,
Through the trials of love, in the thick of despair,
For love's meaning lies in the act of losing,
Is ever unconditional love's faint voice in eternity lost?

The love that seeks love in return, we find,
It is but a fleeting shadow, a trick of the mind,
Seated in the hurried vows, the promises to fade,
Yet others, unspoken in our hearts, are strongly founded and laid.

Love's fire ignites the divine souls, conscious and strong,
Guiding them through perils, where the fire may belong,
More than requited love ever could provide,
In love's sacred flame, the divinity finds its stride.

The divine souls make no promises, yet strong they stand,
Fulfilling those unsaid vows, hand in hand,
Traversing the conscious path, the heavenly beings own,
Born from the eternal fire, love's truth is known.

In this journey to fulfill the divine's decree,
Love's essence, the core of what it means to be free,
Through the trials, through the tears, the consciousness
      evolves and transcends,
For in the fire of love, the divine souls fulfill
      the ethereal mandate that mends.

Bards of Divine Wisdom

Storms in eyes, veiled as tranquil seas they seem,
Hiding fires mighty, hearts ignite in dreams,
Creating sparks, relentless and untamed,
Kindling souls, inextinguishable, unnamed.

Flickers burn, the malevolence they sear,
From the ashes, righteousness shall appear,
Bards of the eternal fire, love's sweet song,
Mitigate the pain of indifference, strong.

Is it a panacea for universal strife,
Or fortitude in the tapestry of life?
An illusion or true resilience found,
In integrity, with fortitude, earthbound.

Strength, a reflection of the soul's grand flight,
Destined to rise in eternal divine light,
Seeking guidance from the Creator's hand,
Each soul rekindles across the land.

For the canvas of humanity to adore,
The holy grail, love at its very core,
Souls aflame with wisdom, divine and bright,
Universal consciousness, the eternal light.

In creation's embrace, forever entwined,
Humanity's flames, in fame, they're defined,
Expanding realms, both seen and concealed,
Soul and universe eternally revealed.

Worlds created, destroyed, recreated, seen,
In silence, the unspoken's enchanting mystery,
Eternal wisdom's whispers, in silence, reside,
Bards of the divine, in magnificence, gleam and guide.

Prerona Mukherjee

I have loved telling stories since I was a little child. While stories spill out of my mind incessantly, only a few find their way into written words. My poems are thoughts, dreams, and feelings captured in words; confessions, and confidences I cannot make. I was born in Aleppo, Syria; I grew up in Calcutta, India; I spent my youth in Edinburgh, United Kingdom. Like the wild parrots and the sea lions, somehow I found my way to San Francisco, and there I stayed. My poems are about the loss of home, the longings of the exiled, and the tax of the road.

Thanatophobia

My father died suddenly; without a will.
I know he was too scared of dying
To grapple with mortality
And such small practical matters

Nevertheless, I got so much from my father.
Once on a visit to Edinburgh,
He gave me his beautiful camera,
And said, you can see a picture everywhere.

He gave me his penchant for drama,
I got his dreamy passion for history.
He gave me his desperate discontent,
I got his irrational, jealously guarded fears.

He loaned me what became my favorite book
About a lost writer who meanders through Bengal
I got the peculiar shape of his nails,
And the easy tears in his eyes.

I had his hunger for more in friendship.
He gave me his incurable story-lust.
His idealization of humble simplicity
And I got his awe of being good.

A sticky memory for almost any song,
Rivaling fear and passion for his father,
A bundle of family stories,
And his ambition to be good

I got all his addictions, including to life.
He gave me his fear of illness, by and by.
But then, when he died, I found
He had left me his terror of death.

Immigrants Lament

She called me an immigrant.
The label jars, pricking my skin.
I belong to a faraway land and,
I wandered far from home; I never left

There is an elastic tie
Between my heart and my home
It pulls me back when I stray too far
Or when I am away too long.

At night, I close my eyes,
And I walk through the streets I love.
The colors of my dreams
Are indigo and scarlet.

My heart cries for home
But where would I go?
My beloved, my Calcutta,
Is not a real place anymore.

The stern old men draped in white
Young cricket players usurping lanes
The boy selling wooden flutes, with mournful eyes
The busy fish seller on the sidewalk.

The sudden rain,
that washes out all sorrow
The crows that dry themselves
on the palm tree near my house.

The orphaned dogs and cats
That rule the nights,
And the strange howls and
Songs that often ring out from them.

The beautiful houses, fading in decay,
The trees that burst through walls,
The Metrorail that was once new and so exciting,
But now even that is old.

The massive Ballygunge Circular Road,
Dotted with roadside bonfires at night.
The proud Southern Avenue,
Striped by a grey-haired park.

The romance of the late afternoon breeze
The passion for tea. The arguments and poetry
The spontaneous social interruptions
The accidental intimacies

The nosy neighbors, the unexpected guest,
The buzzing days and nights, the chatty stranger
The hum of a collective, a people living out loud.
The ebullient life—spilling over from private to public spaces.

These memories are the colors of my dreams.
These images are the shades of my heart.
If you have never loved a place, you will not understand
A place is just a place—if you are not in love.

Yet my heart keeps crying for home.
I am learning to soothe myself.
I tell my heart I am my home…
Like a tortoise—wherever I am.

Dreams

I float in my dreams like a bubble.
I brush against reality.
I break.

I lose myself in the past, like an old love,
I meet a ghost I forgot.
I turn and run.

I dive fathoms deep, in the ocean within
My shadow darts on the surface of my frozen eyes…
I gasp. I'm awake

I quiver like a dew drop cupped in a mirror-maze of lives before
Life's reflection peers into life's tessellation
The spell breaks, I evaporate

The Eucalyptus Tree

A fickle fog flirts
with the hilltop forests.
A few unprovenanced parrots,
That irreverently prospered,
Immigrant trees that grew like grass,
Imposters - no good for wood!
Off with their heads…
Don't steal our food!
This land we were given by our God
Ours by destiny, or because
those that came before us
were not good enough…
nor their gods, compared to ours.
Or maybe they, like the trees and the parrots,
were beneath us in sophistry.

In the moment

Arrive where you are
Bring everywhere you have been
And everyone you used to be
And all that you have loved
Abandon the names and distinctions
The Kingdom of Houses of Cards
This moment, this life, is all we have
This moment, this life, is all we need
You are you and I am me
And yet we are all the same
We cry, we laugh, our hearts melt and burn
And each morning, we start again

Jai Polepalli

Jai Polepalli was raised in Hyderabad. He writes in three languages- English, Telugu and Urdu. In recent times he has been predominantly writing in Urdu. Jai is a neuroscientist by training, and in his own words, "poetry is a perfect complement to the methodical pursuit of scientific knowledge."

अपोह

दो-पहर की धूप में
गुलमोहर की छाँव में
तेरे बे-लिबस बदन पे
बिलोर के बूंदों में
रौशनी देखा
फिर
नूर देखा
पेड़ देखा
पसीना देखा
और
तेरा बदन

जूतों का शबिस्तां

हर रात बिछता है इनका बिस्तर
जहाँ पड़ता नहीं तारों का साया
लहराते नहीं चाँदनी के दरिया
बस एक कोयल की मीठी चीक
गूँजती है सदा बनकर
एक कंदील से पिघलती मोम
की गर्मी तापती है क़बा बनकर
ये चार नंगे दीवारों के बीच
है इन् जूतों का शबिस्तां

कुछ आरज़ू पहले, कुछ नींदों से पहले
खेल रही थी ये फर्श होली मिटटी से
ले कर आये थे जो
सितम-गाह नादान
कुँदल कुँदल कर घर कूज़ागरों के

अब पीता है हर रतगुज़ार
वो ही तमाशा-ए-ख़ाक से
सज बैठी है जो ज़माने में उस कोने में
बुजती हुई प्यास पैरों के उंगलियों की
इन जूतों के ख़्वाबों में
एक मीना बनकर
एक कूज़ा बनकर

अफ़सुर्दा

ग़लत वक़्तों में रहते हैं
घड़ी घर के सारे
मेरे
एक कमरे से दुसरे में जाता हूँ
लिबाज़-ओ-अंदाज़ बदल जाते हैं
मेरे

ग़लत रास्तों में भटकाते हैं
सड़क मोहल्ले के सारे
मेरे
घर से निकलता हूँ
तो पहुँच जाता हूँ घर
मेरे

ग़लत फूल खिलते हैं
बस्ती के नाली में
मेरे
बिछाए बीज नील कमल के
बहाए लेकिन नीलोफ़र आंसू
मेरे

ग़लत खुशियां क़ब्ज़ा
रहती हैं ज़हन में
मेरे
तेरे निगाहों का आशिक़ मैं
ज़र्द-ए-ज़हन है मशरूफ कहीं और
मेरे

ग़लत वक़्त पर
ग़लत गलियों में
ग़लत फूलों के तोड़ने
चल पड़ता है मन
तो तुम रोक लेती हो
इस बदन को
मेरे

Vidur Sahdev

Vidur believes that "poetry is the simplest way of expressing that which is felt intensely in the moment, which if not poured out, would pass away as a fleeting feeling, unsaid and forgotten forever." He shares his writings and thoughts on his blog at **vidursahdev.wordpress.com**.

The Sea

she alluringly beckons
and i slowly walk towards her,
the serenity, the calm, magical
as i reach her grainy shore,

every now and then
her waves flirting in a seductive practiced move,
teasing me to step a little further
into her owned hunting zone,

and i become a captive
with each advancing footstep of mine,
as it sinks effortlessly into the moist hold
of her warm melting sands,

my eyes captivated
by her exquisite beauty
and its wide overpowering expanse,
while my thoughts drowning in her mysterious
unfathomable depths,

the music of her waves splashing
an intoxicating mesmerizing melody
awakening once more the ears
which had been deadened by the irrelevant cacophony
of noisy bustling urban life,

all senses felt soothed as if by a soulful balm,
tranquillity was probably
a word coined,
to define this very feeling
which i felt in that now,

i slowly walk along
the mind a runaway horse
imagining a home built
on this serene yet effervescent shore,
imagining an existence of permanence
on a land where nothing is ever sure,

the moon, a mind reader
hearing the voices in my head,
comes out from behind the clouds
in full glory, owning the skies,
outshining the shiny little stars,
and she succumbs as she always did
to the gravitational powers
of her jealous lover, the moon,
conscious of its presence
her flirtations with me seem over,
as she commands her rising tides
to force me back, and reclaim her ground
intentional machinations to please
the eyes of her watchful celestial lover,

but my feet had sunk too deep to withdraw
and i fell on my back,
somewhat drowned, and yet somewhat alive
resigned to a destiny of being another grain of sand,
another added to those
who had walked on this dreamy land before,
but today, and forever will lie as fallen stars
the scattered grains that make her shore.

The Road Ahead

i walk
like a recently freed man,
enjoying the space
of my heart,
the clutter cleared...
the walls repaired...
repainted
with a new shade
of crimson,
that bubbles
with enthusiasm,
heightened
by the oxygen inhaled
from the colours
of spring air,

a space
reclaimed,
after what seems
an age,
by the original owner
who apparently
himself
had forgotten
the deed of lease,
signed
to this little
valuable space
in his very own name,

to be his
till perpetuity,
or years of breath.
a space—
now free
from all—
legal
or illegal
trespassers,
and rent free
thankless
noisy tenants,
alongwith
their accompanying
clutter
and unwelcome
baggage,
and wares.

a space—
now empty,
yet full,
of life,
which can't
be seen
but can
be felt,
the walls bare,
except for
the pulsating network
of semi visible
invisible veins

which keep
the walls warm,
decorated,
alive
with a rich
rejuvenated
constantly flowing
watery red,

from somewhere
in this
seeming emptiness,
my hand reaches out
to magically pull up
a comfy chair,
and i sink into it,
much
like a stone
happily rushing
to find
the comforting arms
of a waiting
river bed,

home at last
from a series
of life's sagas
and tiring
sojourns,
something gained,
and something lost,
though the sum

of it all
seems to break
all hereto
conventionally established
principles
of maths,

the sum
as it adds herein,
curls up
into a cushion
of experience,
and cradles gently
the tired neck,
keeping
a constant
teacherly check,
on the incessant
on-goings
inside
the numerous
mysterious
tunnels of the head,

and calmed
and comforted
i drift away slowly,
on a boat
without a rudder,
without oars,
or a sail,
into an ocean

of possible,
impossible,
destinations
and adventures,
free—
once again,
to revisit
those lost islands
of dreams,
and
of realities,
I always knew
I could have had.

The Flower

I fall in love with a flower
knowing the temporariness
of her existence
and the uncertain
length of mine,
I don't need a reason
and I don't look for one
for if love could be explained
I'd have no need
for a heart,
she gives nothing
and yet
I receive so much,
balances can be measured
when mounted on scales,
but in this imbalance
that exists
neither of us
is a loser,

I fall in love with a flower
knowing I don't own a vase,
knowing
that there is more
which gives her
her earthen fragrance
and her myriad colours,
than stagnant water
in a captive jar ever could,

I admire her inborn wisdom
of knowing that the bee
is no ordinary thief,

and sometimes
letting go of a part of you,
is necessary
for the continuity
of a larger existence,

I fall in love with a flower
each time I see her,
an elixir to my eyes
a balm to my soul
a being existing in peace
nonchalant to her own beauty,
seeking neither her reflections
nor needing to reflect anyone else,
simply content
under the boundless sky
for her this
momentary presence,

I linger
for as long as I can
before I make my way back,
I fell in love with a flower
and it feels good
to be able to feel that,
for even when time
has weathered us down,
some roots
when watered
can bloom forever.

Honey

the bee
a stealthy thief
or a gentle
romantic lover,
a seeker
in search,
or just another
predictable, ordinary
nectar digger,
the flower
a seemingly
innocent,
yet energetically
vivacious
player,
or an intentionally
beckoning
bewitching
culpable lover,
who is to tell
the story
of them two,
for their dance
of existence
goes far beyond
this temporary
me and you,
with neither seeking
to be shown
as any lesser or greater
than the other,
nor to be reduced
or disempowered

by any imbecile
confining
coined human definitions,
or be governed
by any social
or man-made laws
of artificially fenced
bordered gardens,
for nature is
what nature is,
one, a stinger
and the other
a disarming charmer,
one, a worker, loyal to his queen's mission,
the other
a free sun-loving seducer,
one, a petty thief
and the other
a generous willing giver,

and though
they meet
pretending
to exist
for the continuance
of this sweet life,
but one to one
(honey, i know),
they only exist
to be
with each other.

My Honey Bee

I had always
marvelled
at the sweetness
of the bee,
for she
worked hard
all day,
flower to flower
collecting nectar,
and then
so generously
converting it into
the sweet elixir
of an unparalleled
honey,

i had marvelled
at how giving
a nature,
nature
had given her,
until the day
i met her
in the blooming
spring garden
for a little
tête-à-tête
about a future beyond
those seasonal flowers,

i'd thought
our encounter
would head
in a way,
the way...
where
one might say,
the sweetest
honey lay,

but
she left me
with a sting,
and a resultant
unscratchable
itch,
by which
her...
i'll forever
remember.

The Last Poem

if this were the last poem i write
(for there will always be one
which by choice, design or fate
will one day be that one),
would i still sing the same song
that my words have always sung,

would i happily raise a toast
to this journey of umpteen heartbeats
which passionately beat throughout
irrespective of the prevailing weather,
giving solace in the silences
which the senses often absorbed like a sponge,

would i write about the bittersweet
sense of satisfaction
as i look at the image in the mirror,
a work still in progress
yet complete in the moment
like an unfinished poem
with a waiting completed inevitable last verse,

would i write about the light
which often streamed in like magic
through the often lingering melancholic clouds,
to fall down through my soul's skies
like little crystals of shiny
rejuvenating raindrops,

would i write about how water
rejuvenated me in every way it exists,
a dewdrop, a teardrop, a raindrop,
a trickle, a flow, a sip, a gulp,
and sometimes in the ecstatic way
of an extended, held, savoured breath
whenever i happened to find
myself touched by the saltiness of the sea,

would i write about the untethered bond
between the sky and the earth,
and unabashedly attempt to add
to its essence our presence,
and raise it to an even higher level
by comparing it to a you and i
as one being one, and the other the other,

would i write about the tree
which lovingly always gave refuge
in its shade,
and food in its fruit,
stayed strong beside me
like an inseparable friend
irrespective of the punishing winds
which often made me tremble
but taught me the significance of roots,

would i write about my affection
and my gratitude towards those
that held me close irrespective of the times
they extended beyond the boundaries of their own comfort zones,
about my admiration for the completeness
of those generous beings
whom i learnt to see and value
beyond the selfishness of my own apparent needs,

would i think of writing about the past
which really doesn't matter anymore,
or would i write about a future
which like in a game of chance
could also give me a miss,
or would i happily in the moment
smile like never before,
to celebrate each ray of silent sunshine
that has reached me, touched me, warmed me, grown me
and still continually does,

and so
maybe for once
i'll just let the unwritten words
be a poem,
that last poem birthed,
written in the air of silence
with the ink of gratitude,
for one, for all
and for this shared inexplicable experience
of life
on this spinning earth.

Asif Shahid

Working in development of distributed query processing with 26 years of experience. Interested in hindi and urdu poetry and songs written, sung by giants of Indian cinema.

One

दाग़ दुनिया ने दिये, ज़ख्म ज़माने से मिले
हमको तोहफे ये तुम्हें दोस्त बनाने के मिले

daag duniya ne diye, zakhm jamane se mile
hamko tohfe ye tumhe dost banane ke mile

I got blames and wounds from the world
these were the gifts I got for having you as a friend.

Two

हम तरसते ही, तरसते ही, तरसते ही रहे,
वो फलाने, फलाने से, फलाने से मिले

*ham tarsate hi, tarsate hi, tarsate hi rahe,
wo falane, falane se, falane se mile*

I kept desperately yearning for you
and you met every body except me!

Three

खुद से मिल जाते तो चाहत का भरम रह जाता
क्या मिले आप जो लोगों के मिलाने से मिले

khud se mil jate to chahat ka bharam rah jata
kya mile aap jo logo ke milane se mile

If you had met me on your own volition
then at least there would have been an impression of love
(even if not really) What's the point if you were persuaded
by others to meet me?

Four

कभी लिखवाने गये खत, कभी पढवाने गये
हम हँसिनो से इसी हिले-बहाने से मिले

kabhi likhwane gaye khat, kabhi padhwane gaye
ham hasino se isi hile-bahane se mile

Sometimes I went to meet using excuse to get a (love) letter written
And sometimes to get it read,
These were the excuses I used to meet beauties.

Five

इक नया ज़ख्म मिला, इक नई उमरा मिली
जब किसी शहर में कुछ यार पुराने से मिले

ik nya zakhm mila, ik nai umra mili
jab kisi shahar me kuch yaar purane se mile

I got a new wound and hence a new life
When in some city I met my old friends.

Six

एक हम ही नहीं फिरते हैं किस्सा-ए-ग़म के लिए
उनके खामोश लबो पर भी फ़साने से मिले

ek ham hi nahi firte hai liye kissa-e-gham
unke khamosh labo par bhi fasane se mile

It is not only me who is carrying the burden/story of
Our tragic love saga on my lips
I found that even her quiet lips were telling the story.

Seven

कैसे माने के उन्हें भूल गया तू ऐ कैफ
उनके खत आज हमें तेरे सिरहाने से मिले

kaise maane ke unhe bhul gya tu ae kaif
unke khat aaj hame tere sirhane se mile

How do we believe that you have forgotten her, Kaif
We found letters from her near your head rest.

        Kaif Bhopali

Topaz

I have been through a lot, not quite the same as I've done a lot, because most of my experiences have been from the nose-bleed bleachers. Except for being a poet, being a DJ, and being homeless. Oh, and walking across the United States. And a head-on collision with a 16 wheeler. That's about it. Did I mention poetry? The words I write are self psy-alms, ways of helping my mind synch up with the times, while staying within the shadow of sanity and spirit. For more information and to view my books, please visit poeticphonetics.com.

Grace

When I was a young boy,
The Winds they spoke to me.
Whispered into my ears,
the secrets of the willow trees.
Now I'm not much older,
but a tougher road I walk.
The Winds always around me,
reminding me of our first talks.

Grace grants, grants Grace!
Flower and Bloom, Beauty Creates.
Where there is life to be lived, appreciate!

Dizzy from the noise,
of the loud and busy city,
underneath the chaos,
I hear hushed tones of greenery.
It's really no surprise to find
all living things can talk,
telling stories of creation,
The Wind echoing these thoughts.

Grace grants, grants Grace!
Flower and Bloom, Beauty Creates.
Where there is life to be lived, appreciate!

Cold and lonely evening, long walk home,
hearing hymns of praise that shake my bones.
Rhythms of Nature, smells of The Sea,
reminding me of One Heart, effortlessly.

Grace grants, grants Grace!
Flower and Bloom, Beauty Creates.
Where there is life to be lived, appreciate!

Phantom Prophet

Once, a ghost face whispered
voodoo on my soul,
proclaiming me a skin walker,
with heart as black as coal
that means this flesh is not my flesh,
these bones are not my bones
maybe that's why this restless spirit
never feels at home
Whose body have I stolen? Whose dreams cast into flame?
Am I the individual at fault? Is society to blame?
Answer rebounds from ambient sound
Forbidding questions formed, demanding ego rage and storm
Yet silence forms the heartbeat
The pulse First Nations' drum
These bones are not your bones,
yet their safety you must keep
This flesh is not your flesh,
A Guardian, learn to be
A chant for all relations very different today
Though red and yellow, black and white
Together we must pray
Ancestors voices harmonize with seventh generation
Guiding dancer's steps, rebuilding tradition
So what if I'm a skin walker
These bones are not my bones
this land is not my land
The blessing?
This war is not my war.
I turn my ears to sacred song
I turn my heart to culture.

Leaves Rustle, Heavy is the Root of Light

I tapped the ground as demons danced
Waltzing through my thoughts
Wisdom of the ages
Dripping from their bloody jaws
How did Buddha tame them?
These waves of light and words.
Working, playing, exercising?
Just sitting still is what I heard.
While bode he tree
flames arose
Pyre of perennial plumage
Red, yellow, hallowed orange
Embryonic portals, here, there and gone
Sights and smells, doors to autumn
Life isn't a trick question
It's wrong to not try at all
Mantras, mudras, poems
fine tune creator meant-all
Yet some puzzles still unsolved,
For instance, is the wisest lama
from Peru or from Nepal?

The Power of Monks

A new mother board what should it be?
Linux or Windows as the OS scheme
It's easy to win dough, you just gotta show
Doc, you meant it, per version
Of aboriginal intention to dignify balance
In tales of the fair-he, ball meant dance
Bequeathing victory, therefore to her*
Through the course of the night Yggdrasil whispers
Only with Hel the root can a cola be higher
I ain't lyin' live in the home of the brave
If flow is interrupted, then I'm only a knave
Truth will tell, proof against all spells
Like a boom, I rang universal bell
In da showtao of da sun, Truth
ain't no mist
ain't no terra
ain't no sea
Without being exist, in other words Lie-Nix
No spaghetti code mess, no linguistic programming
In hopes of dethroning, the word
At the pinnacle of pineal gland
It's right there G-land
Middle-earth, Midgard where all more-tells stand
You're a king? Let's see you re-gal
Court the god-is again!

*To quote a common theme
of Fred Ass-stare and Ginger Rogers
now there's no need to crinkle your brain
check it—indigo, holy would be royalty
yet colors of aum, autumn, the same

To travel through time
on the ethereal plane
truths from way back then
some find savory to taste

so if you're feeling heated
soul hasn't been defeated
hibernate your higher self
meditate in a cave

no coincidence Shaolin still known today
it's no secret, vibration, Ch'an, form
the same hand that claps
becomes Buddha's palm

expansive mind loses rhythmic time
springing forward, power knows its own season
be here now, not blinded by another's vision
the dharma of doing, c'est raison d'etre.

Vishal Vatnani

Vishal Vatnani lives in the San Francisco Bay Area and likes to write poetry in English on the topics of love, dystopia, and existentialism. His literary influence comes from Charles Bukowski. Find him on Instagram @vishalvatnani

Something about the evening

Something about the reflecting sunlight,
through the glass doors, turning the store bright.
Something about the color orange,
tells me I'm in the wrong place at the wrong time.

The sidewalk is wet, something is not right.
No clouds in the sky, no water for me.
It's only sold in exchange for dollars,
yet the road is wet, for free, someone cried.

The deep orange of the deep evening,
hits my eye, face to face we come, the sun and I.
Pushing metal carts in and out,
I'm fatigued, and the asphalt keeps melting.

Feet laden with praises from real leather,
claiming their place in the eyes of the shoppers.
Drenched walls reek of mold.
Some could smell ants, others wore feathers.

The ghastly wind that the evening brings,
reminds me of my isolation forever.
If they don't turn the music up at night,
where will I leave my heart to shrink?

His vest read "security", he is the society's cure.
His tongue rests precisely on the store's palate.
His eyes scan nothing, the customers are his anodyne.
Excellent at his job, he finally makes them insecure.

Beautiful faces

You flirted with the beautiful faces,
 just like you'd test drive all the luxury cars.
The down payment, insurance, coveting eyes of the passerby,
was just too high of a price to pay.

So you never owned the experience,
and kept your distance,
to get the best out of everything,
by not getting everything from that one thing.

You drove on the freeway, thinking you'd know better,
in your ok car, you dreamt of visiting exotic places.
But nobody to go with,
and no fuel of excitement in your heart.

You flirted with the beautiful faces,
driving alone on the highway.
They gazed at your shabby hair.
Do you scare them, make them doubt their lives?

You didn't look like Stephen Curry or somebody
But you looked like somebody they oddly knew from the TV.

Your youth was a depreciating asset,
and your time was running out.
Yet you thought you could do better,
and better, and better, and better.
So you flirted with all the beautiful faces,
as if it was zero liability insurance.
Your time was running out.
But you think they'd name a street after you,
for taking your time,
for keeping your choices,
for a perfect life,
that you saw somebody live.
Yes, it must exist,
it must be true.
It's in the news, in Lil man's lyrics.
It must be true.

www.ingramcontent.com/pod-product-compliance
Lightning Source LLC
Chambersburg PA
CBHW060544080526
44586CB00012B/850